S0-AGT-602

MySQL
Pocket Reference

SECOND EDITION

MySQL
Pocket Reference

George Reese

O'REILLY®

Beijing · Cambridge · Farnham · Köln · Paris · Sebastopol · Taipei · Tokyo

MySQL Pocket Reference, Second Edition
by George Reese

Copyright © 2007, 2003 George Reese. All rights reserved.
Printed in Canada.

Published by O'Reilly Media, Inc., 1005 Gravenstein Highway North,
Sebastopol, CA 95472.

O'Reilly books may be purchased for educational, business, or sales
promotional use. Online editions are also available for most titles
(*safari.oreilly.com*). For more information, contact our corporate/
institutional sales department: (800) 998-9938 or *corporate@oreilly.com*.

Editor: Andy Oram
Production Editor:
    Laurel R.T. Ruma
Copyeditor: Genevieve d'Entremont
Proofreader: Laurel R.T. Ruma

Indexer: Johnna VanHoose Dinse
Cover Designer: Karen Montgomery
Interior Designer: David Futato

Printing History:

February 2003:	First Edition.
July 2007:	Second Edition.

Nutshell Handbook, the Nutshell Handbook logo, and the O'Reilly logo are
registered trademarks of O'Reilly Media, Inc. The *Pocket Reference* series
designations, *MySQL Pocket Reference*, the image of a kingfisher, and
related trade dress are trademarks of O'Reilly Media, Inc.

Many of the designations used by manufacturers and sellers to distinguish
their products are claimed as trademarks. Where those designations appear
in this book, and O'Reilly Media, Inc. was aware of a trademark claim, the
designations have been printed in caps or initial caps.

While every precaution has been taken in the preparation of this book, the
publisher and author assume no responsibility for errors or omissions, or for
damages resulting from the use of the information contained herein.

ISBN-10: 0-596-51426-3
ISBN-13: 978-0-596-51426-6
[TM]

Contents

MySQL Pocket Reference

Introduction

When I fly across the country, I often pass the hours programming on my PowerBook. If that programming involves MySQL, I inevitably end up lugging around the book I co-wrote, *Managing and Using MySQL* (O'Reilly). I don't carry around the book to show it off; the problem is that no matter how experienced you are with MySQL, you never know when you will need to look up the exact syntax of an obscure function or SQL statement.

The *MySQL Pocket Reference* is a quick reference that you can take with you anywhere you go. Instead of racking your brain for the exact syntax of a variant of ALTER TABLE that you generally never use, you can reach into your laptop case and grab this reference. As an experienced MySQL architect, administrator, or programmer, you can look to this reference.

This book does not, however, teach MySQL. I expect that you have learned or are in the process of learning MySQL from a book such as *Managing and Using MySQL*. Though I start with a reference on MySQL setup, it is designed to help you remember the full process of MySQL configuration—not to teach you the process.

Acknowledgments

I first would like to thank my editor Andy Oram, as always, for helping me along. I would also like to thank the book's strong technical reviewers, Paul Dubois, Judith Myerson, and Tim Allwine. Finally, I would like to thank my co-authors for *Managing and Using MySQL*, Tim King and Randy Jay Yarger, who helped set the foundation that made this pocket reference possible and necessary.

Conventions

The following conventions are used in this book:

Constant width

> Used to indicate anything that might appear in a program, including keywords, function names, SQL commands, and variable names. This font is also used for code examples, output displayed by commands, and system configuration files.

Constant width bold

> Used to indicate user input.

Constant width italic

> Used to indicate an element (e.g., a filename or variable) that you supply.

Italic

> Used to indicate directory names, filenames, program names, Unix commands, and URLs. This font is also used to introduce new terms and for emphasis.

MySQL 5

If you have been using MySQL for a while, you really don't need to learn a thing about MySQL 5 to keep going. Everything you are used to using still works just as it always has. For the most part, MySQL 5 is about adding enterprise database features seen in other database engines without burdening MySQL with concepts that make it harder to learn and use.

Views

Views are denormalized, table-like structures that represent a snapshot of your data that match specific query parameters. You can thus represent as data from a single table the result of a complex join. New commands supporting views include CREATE VIEW, DROP VIEW, and ALTER VIEW.

Triggers

A database trigger is functionality that you create that gets executed whenever a specific event occurs on a table. For example, you can trigger behavior for a table whenever a new row is inserted. New commands supporting triggers include CREATE TRIGGER and DROP TRIGGER.

Stored Procedures

Stored procedures are the big feature most people have been waiting for. A stored procedure is much like creating a function that is written entirely in SQL and stored in the database. Stored procedures are useful for encapsulating a number of SQL statements that always get executed together under a single logical name for use by clients. MySQL includes a number of new commands to support stored procedures:

- CREATE PROCEDURE
- ALTER PROCEDURE
- DROP PROCEDURE
- CALL
- BEGIN/END

Cursors

A cursor is a tool that enables you to represent an entire data set within a MySQL stored procedure. MySQL cursors are limited in that they are asensitive (a quality affecting their response to changes in the table), nonscrolling (cursors must be used sequentially, moving forward), and read-only. New commands supporting cursors include OPEN, FETCH, and CLOSE.

New Storage Engines

The most common storage engines (also known as table types) in MySQL are MyISAM and InnoDB. But a number of new ones were added in recent versions of MySQL:

ARCHIVE
Offers fast stores and selects without indexes, but no updates or deletions.

BLACKHOLE
Discards data; used to support replication.

CSV
Stores data in a comma-separated values format commonly used for plain text data exchange.

FALCON
A new general-purpose data storage engine that may one day replace InnoDB. It is currently somewhat experimental.

FEDERATED
Offers access to a database on a remote server.

MERGE
Combines multiple MyISAM tables.

NDB/NDBCLUSTER
Network database, used with MySQL Cluster.

Database Events

Introduced with MySQL 5.1, database events allow you to arrange for SQL that runs at a specified time in the future either once, or on a recurring calendar.

Setup

You can install MySQL by compiling the source code with the options that best suit your needs, or by downloading and installing a prebuilt binary. In general, you'll want to use the package management system (such as the BSD ports system) appropriate to your operating system. You can also find both binary and source code at the MySQL web site, *http://www. mysql.com*.

Before installing using either approach, you need to prepare your operating system for MySQL. Specifically, you should create a *mysql* user and group under which MySQL will run.

Downloading MySQL

MySQL AB changes the download process somewhat frequently, so the exact process of downloading MySQL may vary from the details described here. MySQL comes in *standard* and *debug* packages. When in doubt, get the standard package. It is generally what you will want for a production server.

If you are having runtime problems with your MySQL environment, you can test your application against a Debug install to get detailed debug information on your MySQL operation. *You do not want to use the Debug package for any production environment.*

The MySQL download page also provides a variety of additional tools, including test suites, client utilities, libraries, and header files. These tools are not essential to getting

MySQL up and running, though they may be necessary for programming on a machine without a MySQL server installation or just to make life easier.

Configuration

MySQL has three different kinds of configuration, both for the server process at server startup and for the client processes when a user executes them. In order of preference, these configuration options include:

1. Command-line options
2. Configuration file options
3. Environment variable options

In other words, if you have the password option specified on the command line, in your configuration file, and in an environment variable, the command-line option wins. Table 1 shows a list of configuration options. Each option applies to one or more MySQL tools, depending on the context.

Table 1. MySQL configuration options

Option	Description
basedir=*directory*	Specifies the root directory of your MySQL installation.
Batch	Executes in batch mode, meaning no command-line prompts or other information is sent to stdout. This is the default mode when used with a pipe.
character-sets-dir=*directory*	Specifies where your character set files are stored.
Compress	Tells the client and server to use compression in the network protocol.
datadir=*directory*	Specifies the location of MySQL's data files.
debug=*options*	Specifies a list of debug options.

Table 1. MySQL configuration options (continued)

Option	Description
Force	Indicates that you want processing to continue for client utilities even when an error is encountered.
host=*hostname*	Identifies the host to which a client should connect by default.
language=*language*	Specifies the language to use for localization.
password=*password*	Specifies a default password for clients to use to connect.
port=*port_#*	Specifies the port number to which the server should listen and to which clients should connect.
Silent	Silently exit if a connection failure occurs.
skip-new-routines	Tells the MySQL server to avoid new, potential buggy routines.
sleep=*seconds*	Sleep between commands.
socket=*name*	Socket file to use for local connections.
user=*username*	Specifies the user name to use for client connections.
variable-name =*value*	Sets the specified variable name to a particular value.
Verbose	Tells MySQL to talk more about what is happening.
Wait	Tells the client to wait after a connection failure and then retry the connection.

A MySQL configuration file has the following format:

```
# Example MySQL configuration file
#
# These options go to all clients
[client]
password        = my_password
port            = 3306
socket          = /var/lib/mysql/mysql.sock
```

```
# These options are specifically targeted at the mysqld
server
[mysqld]
port            = 3306
socket          = /var/lib/mysql/mysql.sock
max_allowed_packet=1M
```

MySQL supports multiple configuration files. As a general rule, it checks files in the following order of preference:

1. User configuration file (Unix only).
2. Configuration file specified through the --defaults-extra-file=*filename* option.
3. A configuration file in the MySQL data directory.
4. The system configuration file.

In all cases except the command-line and user configuration options, the name of the configuration file on Unix is *my.cnf* and on Windows is *my.ini*. A Unix user can override system configuration information by building his own configuration file in *~/.my.cnf*. The system configuration file on a Unix system is */etc/my.cnf*. Windows, on the other hand, has two system configuration locations, in order of preference:

1. *C:\my.cnf*
2. *C:\WINNT\System32\my.cnf*

You can alternately specify a file on the command line using the --defaults-file=*filename* option. This option causes all options specified in other files to be ignored, even if they are not overridden in the file you specify.

Startup

In general, you will want MySQL to begin running when the operating system comes up. How you do this depends on your operating system.

Mac OS X

The modern Mac OS X binary package automatically sets itself up to launch on start. To verify this, you should see a */Library/ StartupItems/MySQLCOM/* directory on your hard drive.

Solaris

The MySQL binary for Solaris does not set itself up as a service to run at startup. It nevertheless sets up a Solaris manifest file in */var/svc/manifest/application/database/mysql.xml*. You should first verify that this file exists. If not, check the MySQL distribution for a Solaris manifest or look on the Internet. To set up MySQL to launch on startup, first verify it is not yet set to run on startup:

```
$ svcs mysql
```

If you see the following:

```
svcs: Pattern 'mysql' doesn't match any instances
STATE          STIME    FMRI
```

The service is not yet installed. To install the service:

```
$ svccfg import /var/svc/manifest/application/database/
mysql.xml
```

One installed, you should see the following:

```
$ svcs mysql
STATE          STIME    FMRI
disabled       Mar_10   svc:/application/database/mysql:
default
```

To start MySQL and have it run on start-up, execute:

```
$ svcadm enable mysql
```

Other Unix

Setting up other variants of Unix is as simple as copying the script *mysql.server* from the source's *support-files* directory to your version of Unix's startup directory and making sure it is executable by *root*. Under FreeBSD, for example, place this script in */usr/local/etc/rc.d*.

Once installed, you should run the *mysql_install_db* tool to set up your databases.

Set the Root Password

After starting the server, and before doing anything else, set a password for the *root* user:

```
mysqladmin -u root password a_good_password
```

Replication

Configuring two MySQL server instances to use replication requires you to set up one as the replication master (i.e., the authoritative database) and the other as a replication slave. Configuration of the server involves nothing more than setting it up for binary logging and specifying a server ID. When you configure a server for binary logging, you are telling it to save all transactions against it to a binary logfile. Slaves can later read this logfile and determine what transactions to replicate into their respective environments.

Master configuration

As just noted, you must set up binary logging on the master for replication to work. You also need to give the server a server ID. All of this is done through the MySQL configuration file:

```
[mysqld]
log-bin=mysql-bin
server-id=1
```

The server ID is an arbitrary integer (pick whatever value you like), but it must be unique across all MySQL servers in your infrastructure. You will also be handing out IDs to the replication slaves.

Slaves must connect to the master using a valid MySQL user with REPLICATION SLAVE privileges. You can either use an existing user or set up a user specifically for replication.

Slave configuration

As with the master, you need to configure the MySQL slave server to have a unique server ID.

With both the slave and master configured with unique IDs and binary logging enabled on the master, you next need to get some basic configuration information from the master. What makes this complicated is that you need to get this information from the master while no updates are occurring. To accomplish this, start a client on the master and enter:

```
mysql> FLUSH TABLES WITH READ LOCK;
Query OK, 0 rows affected (0.30 sec)

mysql> SHOW MASTER STATUS;
+-------------------+----------+--------------+-----------
-------+
| File              | Position | Binlog_Do_DB | Binlog_
Ignore_DB |
+-------------------+----------+--------------+-----------
-------+
| crm114-bin.000044 |       98 |              |
|
+-------------------+----------+--------------+-----------
-------+
1 row in set (0.05 sec)
```

And in another window, while your *mysql* client with the lock is still running, enter:

```
$ mysqldump --master-data -uroot -p DATABASE_TO_REPLICATE
> /var/tmp/master.dump
```

If you need to replicate existing data, you will need to leave the client running *mysql* open so that your lock remains in place while running *mysqldump*. Failure to do so may result in corruption on the slave.

You can then take your dump file to your slave and import the file. Before importing it, however, you should edit the CHANGE MASTER command near the top of the file to include the proper master server, user name, and password. Make sure to retain the position and logfile values!

Once done with your changes, start the slave with the `--skip-slave` option, load the dump file into your slave, start the slave threads, and you are ready to go.

You can use the same master dump to set up any number of slaves.

Command-Line Tools

You can interact with MySQL entirely from the command line. In general, each MySQL command accepts as an argument any appropriate option from the configuration options listed earlier. You prefix any such option with two dashes:

```
mysql --user=username
```

In addition, each of these options has a short form:

```
mysql -uusername
```

To see which options apply to individual commands and their short forms, refer to the manpage for the command in question using the following command:

```
$ man -M/usr/local/mysql/man mysql
```

MySQL provides the following command-line tools:

msql2mysql

> This utility is handy for people converting applications written for mSQL to MySQL. These days, however, few people need this help.

myisamchk

> This tool verifies the integrity of your MyISAM tables and potentially fixes any problems that it detects.

mysql

> The MySQL interactive SQL interpreter. It enables you to execute SQL on the command line. You can span your SQL across any number of lines. The tool executes your SQL when you terminate it with a semicolon or the escape sequence \g.

mysql_upgrade

After you install a new version of MySQL, you can run this utility to examine your tables and make sure they are consistent with your new version of MySQL. You should run this command each time you upgrade MySQL.

mysqladmin

The MySQL administrative interface. Though many of this tool's functions can be accomplished using SQL and the *mysql* command-line utility, it nevertheless provides a quick way to perform an administrative task straight from the Unix command line without entering an SQL interpreter. You can specifically execute the following administrative commands:

create databasename

Creates the specified database.

drop databasename

The opposite of create, this command destroys the specified database.

extended-status

Provides an extended status message from the server.

flush-hosts

Flushes all cached hosts.

flush-logs

Flushes all logs.

flush-status

Flushes all status variables.

flush-tables

Flushes all tables.

flush-threads

Flushes the thread cache.

flush-privileges

Forces MySQL to reload all grant tables.

kill id[,id]
> Kills the specified MySQL threads.

password new_password
> Sets the password for the user to the specified new password. mysqladmin -u root password *new_password* should be the first thing you do with any new MySQL install.

ping
> Verifies that *mysqld* is actually running.

processlist
> Shows the active MySQL threads. You can kill these threads with the mysqladmin kill command.

reload
> Reloads the grant tables.

refresh
> Flushes all tables, closes all logfiles, then opens them again.

shutdown
> Shuts MySQL down.

status
> Shows an abbreviated server status.

variables
> Prints out available variables.

version
> Displays the server version information.

mysqlaccess
> A command-line interface for managing users. This tool is basically a shortcut for the SQL GRANT command.

mysqlcheck
> This tool is a data integrity verifier much like *myisamchk*. A key difference is that you run this tool while MySQL is

running. Exactly what kind of checks and fixes occur vary from database engine to database engine.

mysqld

The MySQL server process. You should never start this directly; instead use *mysqld_safe*.

mysqld_safe

The server process manager. (Under MySQL versions prior to MySQL 4.0, this script was called *safe_mysqld*.) It is a process that starts up the *mysqld* server process and restarts it should it crash. Note that the *mysql.server* startup script executes *mysqld_safe* as the appropriate user at server startup.

mysqldump

Dumps the state of a MySQL database or set of databases to a text file that you can later use to restore the databases you dumped.

mysqlimport

Imports text files in a variety of formats into your database. It expects the base name (the name of the file without its extension) to match the name of the table you will import.

mysqlshow

Displays the structure of the specified MySQL database objects, including databases, tables, and columns.

mysqlslap

A tool to emulate client load on your MySQL server.

Data Types

For each data type, the syntax shown uses square brackets ([]) to indicate optional parts of the syntax. The following example shows how BIGINT is explained in this chapter:

```
BIGINT[(display_size)]
```

This indicates that you can use BIGINT alone or with a display size value. The italics indicate that you do not enter *display_size* literally, but instead enter your own value. Possible uses of BIGINT include:

```
BIGINT
BIGINT(20)
```

In addition to the BIGINT type, many other MySQL data types support the specification of a display size. Unless otherwise specified, this value must be an integer between 1 and 255.

Before MySQL 5, MySQL would silently change column values in certain circumstances. As of MySQL 5, these silent changes no longer happen.

VARCHAR → CHAR

When the specified VARCHAR column size is less than four characters, it is converted to CHAR.

CHAR → VARCHAR

When a table has at least one column of a variable length, all CHAR columns greater than three characters in length are converted to VARCHAR.

TIMESTAMP *display sizes*

Display sizes for TIMESTAMP fields must be an even value between 2 and 14. A display size of 0 or greater than 14 converts the field to a display size of 14. An odd-valued display size is converted to the next highest even value. MySQL 5 no longer takes a size value for timestamps.

Numerics

MySQL supports all ANSI SQL2 numeric data types. MySQL numeric types break down into integer, decimal, and floating point types. Within each group, the types differ by the amount of storage required for them.

Numeric types allow you to specify a display size, which affects the way MySQL displays results. The display size bears no relation to the internal storage provided by each data type. In addition, the decimal and floating point types allow you to optionally specify the number of digits that follow the decimal point. In such cases, the digits value should be an integer from 0 to 30 that is at most two less than the display size. If you do make the digits value greater than two less than the display size, the display size will automatically change to two more than the digits value. For instance, MySQL automatically changes FLOAT(6,5) to FLOAT(7,5).

When you insert a value into a column that requires more storage than the data type allows, it will be clipped to the minimum (negative values) or maximum (positive values) value for that data type. MySQL will issue a warning when such clipping occurs during ALTER TABLE, LOAD DATA INFILE, UPDATE, and multirow INSERT statements. The exception is when you are running MySQL 5 or later under strict SQL mode, in which case MySQL will raise an error for inserts and updates.

The AUTO_INCREMENT attribute may be supplied for at most one column of an integer type in a table. The UNSIGNED attribute may be used with any numeric type. An unsigned column may contain only nonnegative integers or floating-point values. The ZEROFILL attribute indicates that the column should be left padded with zeros when displayed by MySQL. The number of zeros padded is determined by the column's display width.

BIGINT

BIGINT[(*display_size*)] [AUTO_INCREMENT] [UNSIGNED] [ZEROFILL]

Storage

8 bytes

Description

Largest integer type, supporting a range of whole numbers from -9,223,372,036,854,775,808 to 9,223,372,036,854,775,807 (0 to 18,446,744,073,709,551,615 unsigned). Because of the way

MySQL handles BIGINT arithmetic, you should avoid performing any arithmetic operations on unsigned BIGINT values greater than 9,223,372,036,854,775,807. If you do, you may end up with imprecise results.

BIT

BIT[(bits)]

Storage

bits bits + 7 or 8 bits (approximately)

Description

Prior to MySQL 5.0.3, a BIT field behaved exactly like a TINYINT(1) field. This data type stores a bitmap value of the specified number of bits. If you enter a value requiring fewer bits than allowed for the field, MySQL will pad the left bits with zeroes.

DEC

Synonym for DECIMAL.

DECIMAL

DECIMAL[(precision, [scale])] [UNSIGNED] [ZEROFILL]

Storage

Varies

Description

Stores floating-point numbers where precision is critical, such as for monetary values. DECIMAL types require you to specify the precision and scale. The precision is the number of significant digits in the value. The scale is the number of those digits that come after the decimal point. For example, a BALANCE column declared as DECIMAL(9, 2) would store numbers with nine significant digits, two of which are to the right of the decimal point. The range for this declaration would be -9,999,999.99 to 9,999,999.99. If you specify a number with more decimal points, it is rounded to fit the proper scale. Values beyond the range of the DECIMAL are clipped to fit within the range.

Prior to MySQL 5, MySQL actually stores DECIMAL values as strings, not as floating-point numbers. It uses one character for each digit, one character for the decimal points when the scale is greater than 0, and one character for the sign of negative numbers. When the scale is 0, the value contains no fractional part.

ANSI SQL supports the omission of precision and/or scale where the omission of scale creates a default scale of zero and the omission of precision defaults to an implementation-specific value. In the case of MySQL, the default precision is 10.

DOUBLE

DOUBLE[(*display_size*, *digits*)] [ZEROFILL]

Storage

8 bytes

Description

A double-precision floating-point number. This type stores large floating-point values. DOUBLE columns store negative values from -1.7976931348623157E+308 to -2.2250738585072014E-308, 0, and positive numbers from 2.2250738585072014E-308 to 1.7976931348623157E+308.

DOUBLE PRECISION

Synonym for DOUBLE.

FLOAT

FLOAT[(*display_size*, *digits*)] [ZEROFILL]

Storage

4 bytes

Description

A single-precision floating-point number. This type is used to store small floating-point numbers. FLOAT columns can store negative values between -3.402823466E+38 and -1.175494351E-38, 0, and positive values between 1.175494351E-38 and 3.402823466E+38.

INT

INT[(*display_size*)] [AUTO_INCREMENT] [UNSIGNED] [ZEROFILL]

Storage

4 bytes

Description

A basic whole number with a range of -2,147,483,648 to 2,147,483,647 (0 to 4,294,967,295 unsigned).

INTEGER

Synonym for INT.

MEDIUMINT

MEDIUMINT[(*display_size*)] [AUTO_INCREMENT] [UNSIGNED] [ZEROFILL]

Storage

3 bytes

Description

A basic whole number with a range of -8,388,608 to 8,388,607 (0 to 16,777,215 unsigned).

NUMERIC

Synonym for DECIMAL.

REAL

Synonym for DOUBLE.

SMALLINT

SMALLINT[(*display_size*)] [AUTO_INCREMENT] [UNSIGNED] [ZEROFILL]

Storage

2 bytes

Description

A basic whole number with a range of -32,768 to 32,767 (0 to 65,535 unsigned).

TINYINT

```
TINYINT[(display_size)] [AUTO_INCREMENT] [UNSIGNED] [ZEROFILL]
```

Storage

1 byte

Description

A basic whole number with a range of -128 to 127 (0 to 255 unsigned).

Strings

MySQL supports two general string categories: text and binary. Each category, in turn, has different types to support different field sizes and collations. Depending on the collation, MySQL performs string comparisons on a case-sensitive, case-insensitive, or binary (byte-by-byte) basis.

When a text type (CHAR, VARCHAR, etc.) is qualified by the BINARY keyword, that column remains a text column but uses a binary collation.

BINARY

```
BINARY(size)
```

Size

Specified by the size value in a range of 0 to 255.

Storage

size bytes

Description

The BINARY data type is the binary version of the CHAR data type. This main difference is that this field stores binary data and the size is measured by bytes, not characters. Binary values are right padded to the specified field size when the value entered is less than the field size. Starting with MySQL 5.0.15, the pad value is 0x00. In earlier versions, it is a space.

BLOB

Binary form of TEXT.

CHAR

CHAR(*size*) [BINARY] [CHARACTER SET *charset*] [COLLATE *collation*]

Size

Specified by the *size* value in a range of to 255.

Storage

Varies based on the specified size and the underlying character encoding.

Description

A fixed-length text field. String values with fewer characters than the column's size are right padded with spaces. The right padding is removed on retrieval of the value from the database.

CHAR(0) fields are useful for backward compatibility with legacy systems that no longer store values in the column.

CHARACTER

Synonym for CHAR.

CHARACTER VARYING

Synonym for VARCHAR.

LONGBLOB

Binary form of LONGTEXT.

LONGTEXT

LONGTEXT [CHARACTER SET charset] [COLLATE collation]

Size

0 to 4,294,967,295.

Storage

Length of value + 4 bytes.

Description

Storage for large text values. While the theoretical limit on the size of the text that can be stored in a LONGTEXT column exceeds 4 GB, the practical limit is much less due to limitations of the MySQL communication protocol and the amount of memory available to both the client and server ends of the communication.

MEDIUMBLOB

Binary form of MEDIUMTEXT.

MEDIUMTEXT

MEDIUMTEXT [CHARACTER SET charset] [COLLATE collation]

Size

0 to 16,777,215.

Storage

Length of value + 3 bytes.

Description

Storage for medium-sized text values.

NCHAR

Synonym of CHAR.

NATIONAL CHAR

Synonym of CHAR.

NATIONAL CHARACTER

Synonym of CHAR.

NATIONAL VARCHAR

Synonym of VARCHAR.

TEXT

TEXT [CHARACTER SET *charset*] [COLLATE *collation*]

Size
0 to 65,535.

Storage
Length of value + 2 bytes.

Description
Storage for most text values.

TINYBLOB

Binary form of TINYTEXT.

TINYTEXT

TINYTEXT [CHARACTER SET *charset*] [COLLATE *collation*]

Size
0 to 255.

Storage

Length of value + 1 byte.

Description

Storage for short text values.

VARBINARY

VARBINARY(*size*)

Size

Specified by the *size* value.

Storage

size bytes

Description

The VARBINARY data type is the binary version of the VARCHAR data type. This main difference is that this field stores binary data and the size is measured by bytes, not characters. Unlike BINARY values, VARBINARY values are not right padded.

VARCHAR

VARCHAR(size) [BINARY] [CHARACTER SET *charset*] [COLLATE *collation*]

Size

Specified by the *size* value in a range of to 65,532 (1 to 255 prior to MySQL 5). The size is the effective size of the column and is limited by the maximum row size in characters. The actual storage size thus depends on the underlying character set of the column.

Storage

Varies as a function of the number of characters specified by size and the storage requirements of the individual characters in accordance with the underlying character encoding mechanism.

Description

Storage for variable-length text. Trailing spaces are removed from VARCHAR values prior to MySQL 5. MySQL 5 and later follow the standard of not removing trailing whitespaces.

Dates

MySQL date types are extremely flexible tools for storing date information. They are also extremely forgiving in the belief that it is up to the application, not the database, to validate date values. MySQL only checks that months range from 0 to 12 and dates range from to 31. February 31, 2001, is therefore a legal MySQL date. More useful, however, is the fact that February 0, 2001, is a legal date. In other words, you can use 0 to signify dates in which you do not know a particular piece of the date. MySQL 5 is more restrictive on what it will allow in date fields.

Though MySQL is somewhat forgiving on the input format, you should attempt to format all date values in your applications in MySQL's native format to avoid any confusion. MySQL always expects the year to be the leftmost element of a date format. If you assign an illegal value in an SQL operation, MySQL inserts a zero for that value.

MySQL automatically converts date and time values to integer values when used in an integer context.

DATE

DATE

Format
YYYY-MM-DD (2001-01-01)

Storage
3 bytes

Description

Stores a date in the range of January 1, 1000 ('1000-01-01') to December 31, 9999 ('9999-12-31') in the Gregorian calendar.

DATETIME

DATETIME

Format

YYYY-MM-DD hh:mm:ss (2001-01-01 01:00:00)

Storage

8 bytes

Description

Stores a specific time in the range of 12:00:00 A.M., January 1, 1000 ('1000-01-01 00:00:00') to 11:59:59 P.M., December 31, 9999 ('9999-12-31 23:59:59') in the Gregorian calendar.

TIME

TIME

Format

hh:mm:ss (06:00:00)

Storage

3 bytes

Description

Stores a time value in the range of midnight ('00:00:00') to one second before midnight ('23:59:59').

TIMESTAMP

TIMESTAMP

Format

YYYY-MM-DD hh:mm:ss (2001-01-01 01:00:00)

Storage

4 bytes

Description

A simple representation of a point in time down to the second in the range of midnight on January 1, 1970, to one minute before midnight on December 31, 2037. Its primary utility is keeping track of table modifications. When you insert a NULL value into a TIMESTAMP column, the current date and time are inserted instead. When you modify any value in a row with a TIMESTAMP column, the first TIMESTAMP column will be automatically updated with the current date and time.

The timestamp format used prior to MySQL 4.1 is no longer supported in MySQL 5.1.

YEAR

YEAR[(*size*)]

Format

YYYY (2001)

Storage

1 byte

Description

Stores a year of the Gregorian calendar. The size parameter enables you to store dates using 2-digit years or 4-digit years. The range for a YEAR(4) is 1900 to 2155; the range for a YEAR(2) is 1970-2069. The default size is YEAR(4).

Complex Types

MySQL's complex data types ENUM and SET are just special string types. They are listed separately in this book because they are conceptually more complex and represent a lead into the SQL3 data types that MySQL may support in the future.

ENUM

ENUM(*value1*, *value2*, ...)

Storage

1–255 members: 1 byte

256–65,535 members: 2 bytes

Description

Stores one value of a predefined list of possible strings. When you create an ENUM column, you provide a list of all possible values. Inserts and updates are allowed to set the column to values only from that list. Any attempt to insert a value that is not part of the enumeration will cause an empty string to be stored instead.

You may reference the list of possible values by index, where the index of the first possible value is 0. For example:

```
SELECT COLID FROM TBL WHERE COLENUM = 0;
```

Assuming COLID is a primary key column and COLENUM is the column of type ENUM, this statement retrieves the primary keys of all rows in which the COLENUM value equals the first value of that list. Similarly, sorting on ENUM columns happens according to index, not string value.

The maximum number of elements allowed for an ENUM column is 65,535.

SET

SET(value1, value2, ...)

Storage

1–8 members: 1 byte

9–16 members: 2 bytes

17–24 members: 3 bytes

25–32 members: 4 bytes

33–64 members: 8 bytes

Description

A list of values taken from a predefined set of values. A field can contain any number—including none—of the strings specified in the SET statement. A SET is basically an ENUM that allows each field to contain more than one of the specified values. A SET, however, is not stored according to index, but as a complex bit map. Given a SET with the members Orange, Apple, Pear, and Banana, each element is represented by an "on" bit in a byte, as shown in Table 2.

Table 2. MySQL's representation of set elements

Member	Decimal value	Bitwise representation
Orange	1	0001
Apple	2	0010
Pear	4	0100
Banana	8	1000

In this example, the combined values of Orange and Pear are stored in the database as 5 (bits 0101).

You can store a maximum of 64 values in a SET column. Though you can assign the same value multiple times in an SQL statement updating a SET column, only a single value will actually be stored.

SQL

MySQL fully supports ANSI SQL 92, entry level. A SQL reference for MySQL is thus largely a general SQL reference. Nevertheless, MySQL contains some proprietary enhancements that can help you at the *mysql* command line. This section thus provides a reference for the SQL query language as it is supported in MySQL.

SQL is a kind of controlled English language consisting of verb phrases. Each of these verb phrases begins with an SQL command followed by other SQL keywords, literals, identifiers, or punctuation.

Case Sensitivity

Case-sensitivity in MySQL depends on a variety of factors, including the token in question and the underlying operating system. Table 3 shows the case-sensitivity of different SQL tokens in MySQL.

Table 3. The case-sensitivity of MySQL

Token type	Case-sensitivity
Keywords	Case-insensitive.
Identifiers (databases and tables)	Dependent on the case-sensitivity for the underlying operating system. On all Unix systems except Mac OS X using HFS+, database and table names are case-sensitive. On Mac OS X using HFS+ and Windows, they are case-insensitive.
Table aliases	Case-sensitive.
Column aliases	Case-insensitive.

Literals

Literals come in the following varieties:

String

> String literals may be enclosed either by single or double quotes. If you wish to be ANSI compatible, you should always use single quotes. Within a string literal, you may represent special characters through escape sequences. An escape sequence is a backslash followed by another character to indicate to MySQL that the second character has a meaning other than its normal meaning. Table 4 shows the MySQL escape sequences. Quotes within a string can be escaped with doubled apostrophes:
>
> ```
> 'This is a ''quote'''
> ```

Table 4. MySQL escape sequences.

Escape sequence	Value
\0	NUL
\'	Single quote
\"	Double quote
\b	Backspace
\n	Newline
\r	Carriage return
\t	Tab
\z	Ctrl-z (workaround for Windows use of Ctrl-z as EOF)
\\	Backslash
\%	Percent sign (only in contexts where a percent sign would be interpreted as a wildcard)
_	Underscore (only in contexts where an underscore would be interpreted as a wildcard)

However, you do not need to double up on single quotes when the string is enclosed by double quotes.

Binary

Like string literals, binary literals are enclosed in single or double quotes. You must use escape sequences in binary data to escape NUL (ASCII 0), " (ASCII 34), ' (ASCII 39), and \ (ASCII 92).

Bit

Bit values are 1s and 0s enclosed in single quotes and preceded by a b: b'010101', b'10', etc.

Boolean

TRUE and FALSE.

Decimal

Numbers appear as a sequence of digits. Negative numbers are preceded by a - sign and a . indicates a decimal point. You may also use scientific notation, as in: -45198. 2164e+10.

Hexadecimal

> The way in which a hexadecimal is interpreted is dependent on the context. In a numeric context, the hexadecimal literal is treated as a numeric value. In a nonnumeric context, it is treated as a binary value. For example, 0x1 + 1 is 2, but 0x4d7953514c by itself is MySQL.

Null

> The special keyword NULL signifies a null literal in SQL. In the context of import files, the special escape sequence \N signifies a null value.

Identifiers

You can reference any given object on a MySQL server—assuming you have the proper rights—using one of the following conventions:

Absolute naming

> Absolute naming specifies the full path of the object you are referencing. For example, the column BALANCE in the table ACCOUNT in the database BANK would be referenced absolutely as:
>
> ```
> BANK.ACCOUNT.BALANCE
> ```

Relative naming

> Relative naming allows you to specify only part of the object's name, with the rest of the name being assumed based on your current context. For example, if you are currently connected to the BANK database, you can reference the BANK.ACCOUNT.BALANCE column as ACCOUNT. BALANCE. In an SQL query where you have specified that you are selecting from the ACCOUNT table, you may reference the column using only BALANCE. You must provide an extra layer of context whenever relative naming might result in ambiguity. An example of such ambiguity would be a SELECT statement pulling from two tables that both have BALANCE columns.

Aliasing

Aliasing enables you to reference an object using an alternate name that helps avoid both ambiguity and the need to fully qualify a long name.

In general, MySQL allows you to use any character in an identifier. (Older versions of MySQL limited identifiers to valid alphanumeric characters from the default character set, as well as $ and _.) This rule is limited, however, for databases and tables, because these values must be treated as files on the local filesystem. You can, therefore, use only characters valid for the underlying filesystem's naming conventions in a database or table name. Specifically, you may not use / or . in a database or table name. You can never use NUL (ASCII 0) or ASCII 255 in an identifier. MySQL 5 lifts these restrictions.

When an identifier is also an SQL keyword, you must enclose the identifier in backticks:

```
CREATE TABLE 'select' ( 'table' INT NOT NULL PRIMARY KEY
AUTO_INCREMENT);
```

Since Version 3.23.6, MySQL supports the quoting of identifiers using both backticks and double quotes. For ANSI compatibility, however, you should use double quotes for quoting identifiers. You must, however, be running MySQL in ANSI_QUOTES mode.

Comments

You can introduce comments in your SQL to specify text that should not be interpreted by MySQL. This is particularly useful in batch scripts for creating tables and loading data. MySQL specifically supports three kinds of commenting: C, shell-script, and ANSI SQL commenting.

C commenting treats anything between /* and */ as comments. Using this form of commenting, your comments can span multiple lines.

For example:

```
/*
 * Creates a table for storing customer account
information.
*/
DROP TABLE IF EXISTS ACCOUNT;

CREATE TABLE ACCOUNT ( ACCOUNT_ID BIGINT NOT NULL
                       PRIMARY KEY AUTO_INCREMENT,
                       BALANCE DECIMAL(9,2) NOT NULL );
```

Shell-script commenting treats anything from a # character to the end of a line as a comment:

```
CREATE TABLE ACCOUNT ( ACCOUNT_ID BIGINT NOT NULL
                       PRIMARY KEY AUTO_INCREMENT,
                       BALANCE DECIMAL(9,2)
                       NOT NULL ); # Not null ok?
```

MySQL does not really support ANSI SQL commenting, but it comes close. ANSI SQL commenting is distinguished by adding -- to the end of a line. MySQL supports two dashes and a whitespace (--) followed by the comment. The space is the non-ANSI part:

```
DROP TABLE IF EXISTS ACCOUNT; -- Drop the table if it
already exists
```

Commands

This section presents the full syntax of all commands accepted by MySQL.

ALTER DATABASE

ALTER DATABASE *database create_options*

The ALTER DATABASE statement enables you to make changes to the core configuration for a given database schema. You must have ALTER privileges on the target database in order to perform this command.

ALTER SCHEMA is a synonym for ALTER DATABASE.

Examples

```
ALTER DATABASE statistics DEFAULT CHARACTER SET utf8;
```

ALTER EVENT

```
ALTER EVENT
    [DEFINER = { user | CURRENT_USER }] name
    [ON SCHEDULE schedule]
    [RENAME TO new_name]
    [ON COMPLETION [NOT] PRESERVE]
    [ENABLE | DISABLE]
    [COMMENT 'comment string']
    [DO statement]
```

Alters the characteristics associated with the event. For details on the meanings of the various clauses, view the CREATE EVENT command.

ALTER FUNCTION

```
ALTER FUNCTION name
    [{CONTAINS SQL | NO SQL | READS SQL DATA | MODIFIES SQL DATA}]
    [SQL SECURITY { DEFINER | INVOKER}]
    [COMMENT 'comment string']
```

Alters the characteristics associated with the function. The ALTER ROUTINE permission (granted automatically to a procedure creator) is required to make these changes.

ALTER PROCEDURE

```
ALTER PROCEDURE name
    [{CONTAINS SQL | NO SQL | READS SQL DATA | MODIFIES SQL DATA}]
    [SQL SECURITY { DEFINER | INVOKER}]
    [COMMENT 'comment string']
```

Alters the characteristics associated with the procedure. The ALTER ROUTINE permission (granted automatically to a procedure creator) is required to make these changes.

ALTER TABLE

```
ALTER [IGNORE] TABLE table action_list
```

The ALTER statement covers a wide range of actions that modify the structure of a table. This statement is used to add, change, or remove columns from an existing table as well as to remove indexes. To perform modifications on the table, MySQL creates a copy of the table and changes it, meanwhile queuing all table altering queries. When the change is done, the old table is removed and the new table put in its place. At this point the queued queries are performed.

As a safety precaution, if any of the queued queries create duplicate keys that should be unique, the ALTER statement is rolled back and cancelled. If the IGNORE keyword is present in the statement, the ALTER statement proceeds as normal until the first integrity concern.

Possible actions in action_list include:

```
ADD [COLUMN] create_clause [FIRST | AFTER column]
ADD [COLUMN] (create_clause, create_clause,...)
```
Adds a new column to the table. The create_clause is the SQL that would define the column in a normal table creation (see CREATE TABLE for the syntax and valid options). The column will be created as the first column if the FIRST keyword is specified. Alternately, you can use the AFTER keyword to specify which column it should be added after. If neither FIRST nor AFTER is specified, the column is added at the end of the table's column list. You may add multiple columns at once by enclosing multiple create clauses separated with commas, inside parentheses.

```
ADD [CONSTRAINT symbol] FOREIGN KEY name (column, ...)
[reference]
```
Currently applies only to the InnoDB table type, which supports foreign keys. This syntax adds a foreign key reference to your table.

```
ADD FULLTEXT [name] (column, ...)
```
Adds a new full text index to the table using the specified columns.

`ADD INDEX [name] (column, ...)`

Adds an index to the altered table, indexing the specified columns. If the name is omitted, MySQL will choose one automatically.

`ADD PRIMARY KEY (column, ...)`

Adds a primary key consisting of the specified columns to the table. An error occurs if the table already has a primary key.

`ADD UNIQUE[name] (column, ...)`

Adds a unique index to the altered table; similar to the `ADD INDEX` statement.

`ALTER [COLUMN] column SET DEFAULT value`

Assigns a new default value for the specified column. The `COLUMN` keyword is optional and has no effect.

`ALTER [COLUMN] column DROP DEFAULT`

Drops the current default value for the specified column. A new default value is assigned to the column based on the `CREATE` statement used to create the table. The `COLUMN` keyword is optional and has no effect.

`CONVERT TO CHARACTER SET charset [COLLATE collation]`

`[DEFAULT] CHARACTER SET charset [COLLATE collation]`

Converts the column to the specified character set based on the named collation.

`CHANGE [COLUMN] column create_clause`

`MODIFY [COLUMN] create_clause [FIRST | AFTER column]`

Alters the definition of a column. This statement is used to change a column from one type to a different type while affecting the data as little as possible. The create clause is the same syntax as in the `CREATE TABLE` statement. This includes the name of the column. The `MODIFY` version is the same as `CHANGE` if the new column has the same name as the old. The `COLUMN` keyword is optional and has no effect. MySQL will try its best to perform a reasonable conversion. Under no circumstance will MySQL give up and return an error when using this statement; a conversion of some sort will always be performed. With this in mind, you should make a backup of the data before the conversion and immediately check the new values to see if they are reasonable.

DISABLE KEYS

Tells MySQL to stop updating indexes for MyISAM tables. This clause applies only to nonunique indexes. Because MySQL is more efficient at rebuilding its keys than it is at building them one at a time, you may want to disable keys while performing bulk inserts into a database. You should avoid this trick, however, if you have read operations going against the table while the inserts are running.

DISCARD TABLESPACE

When using InnoDB, this will delete the underlying *.idb* file if you are using per-table tablespaces. Be sure to back up the old *.idb* file before issuing this command.

DROP [COLUMN] *column*

Deletes a column from a table. This statement will remove a column and all its data from a table permanently. There is no way to recover data destroyed in this manner other than from backups. All references to this column in indexes will be removed. Any indexes where this was the sole column will be destroyed as well. (The COLUMN keyword is optional and has no effect.)

DROP PRIMARY KEY

Drops the primary key from the table.

DROP INDEX KEY

Removes an index from a table. This statement will completely erase an index from a table. This statement will not delete or alter any of the table data itself, only the index data. Therefore, an index removed in this manner can be recreated using the ALTER TABLE ... ADD INDEX statement.

ENABLE KEYS

Recreates the indexes no longer being updated because of a prior call to DISABLE KEYS.

IMPORT TABLESPACE

Allows you to import the data stored in an *.idb* file from a backup or other source.

ORDER BY *column* [ASC | DESC]

Forces the table to be reordered by sorting on the specified column name. The table will no longer be in this order when new rows are inserted. This option is useful for optimizing tables for common sorting queries. You can specify multiple columns.

RENAME [AS] *new_table*

RENAME [TO] *new_table*

> Changes the name of the table. This operation does not affect any of the data or indexes within the table, only the table's name. If this statement is performed alone, without any other ALTER TABLE clauses, MySQL will not create a temporary table as with the other clauses, but simply perform a fast operating system-level rename of the table files.

table_options

> Enables a redefinition of the tables options such as the table type.

Multiple ALTER statements may be combined into one using commas, as in the following example:

```
ALTER TABLE mytable DROP myoldcolumn, ADD mynewcolumn INT
```

To perform any of the ALTER TABLE actions, you must have SELECT, INSERT, DELETE, UPDATE, CREATE, and DROP privileges for the table in question.

Examples

```
# Add the field 'address2' to the table 'people' and make
# it of type 'VARCHAR' with a maximum length of 100.
ALTER TABLE people ADD COLUMN address2 VARCHAR(100)

# Add two new indexes to the 'hr' table, one regular index
# for the 'salary' field and one unique index for the 'id'
# field. Also, continue operation if duplicate values are
# found while creating the 'id_idx' index
# (very dangerous!).
ALTER TABLE hr ADD INDEX salary_idx ( salary )
ALTER IGNORE TABLE hr ADD UNIQUE id_idx ( id )

# Change the default value of the 'price' field in the
# 'sprockets' table to $19.95.
ALTER TABLE sprockets ALTER price SET DEFAULT '$19.95'

# Remove the default value of the 'middle_name' field in
# the 'names' table.
ALTER TABLE names ALTER middle_name DROP DEFAULT

# Change the type of the field 'profits' from its previous
# value (which was perhaps INTEGER) to BIGINT. The first
```

```
# instance of 'profits' is the column to change, and the
# second is part of the create clause.
ALTER TABLE finances CHANGE COLUMN profits profits BIGINT

# Remove the 'secret_stuff' field from the table
# 'not_private_anymore'
ALTER TABLE not_private_anymore DROP secret_stuff

# Delete the named index 'id_index' as well as the primary
# key from the table 'cars'.
ALTER TABLE cars DROP INDEX id_index, DROP PRIMARY KEY

# Rename the table 'rates_current' to 'rates_1997'
ALTER TABLE rates_current RENAME AS rates_1997
```

ALTER TABLESPACE

```
ALTER TABLESPACE tablespace
 ADD DATAFILE 'file'
 INITIAL_SIZE = size
 ENGINE = engine
ALTER TABLESPACE tablespace
 DROP DATAFILE 'file'
 ENGINE = engine
```

Allows you to change the file structures supporting a given tablespace. The size is a number provided in bytes for the initial size of the tablespace. You may optionally follow the number with an M or a G to indicate megabytes or gigabytes. This command is available only in MySQL 5.1 for NDBCLUSTER tables.

ALTER VIEW

```
ALTER [ALGORITHM = {UNDEFINED | MERGE | TEMPTABLE}]
 [DEFINER = { user | CURRENT_USER }]
 [SQL SECURITY { DEFINER | INVOKER }]
 VIEW name [(columns)]
 AS select_statement
 [WITH [CASCADED | LOCAL] CHECK OPTION]
```

Modifies a view in the database. This method is roughly similar to dropping a view and creating new and requires both CREATE VIEW and DROP privileges.

ANALYZE TABLE

```
ANALYZE TABLE table1, table2, ..., tablen
```

Acquires a read lock on the table and performs an analysis on it for MyISAM, InnoDB, and BDB tables. The analysis examines the key distribution in the table. It returns a result set with the following columns:

Table
    The name of the table.

Op
    The value analyze.

Msg_type
    One of status, error, or warning.

Msg_text
    The message resulting from the analysis.

BEGIN

```
BEGIN [WORK]
[begin_label:] BEGIN statements END [end_label]
```

The first form begins a new transaction. The transaction is committed through the use of the COMMIT statement or a command that forces an implicit commit (such as CREATE TABLE). To rollback a transaction, use the ROLLBACK command.

The second form is unrelated to the first. It indicates that a new series of statements that define a stored procedure. It is preceded by a CREATE PROCEDURE statement. If you use the optional begin label, you must have a matching end label in your END statement. Each statement inside the BEGIN/END must be terminated by a semicolon (;). You must, therefore, alter your delimiter before issuing a BEGIN.

START TRANSACTION is a synonym for the first form of BEGIN.

Examples

```
# Execute a transaction
BEGIN
UPDATE person SET last_name 'Smith' WHERE person_id = 1;
UPDATE address SET city = 'Minneapolis' WHERE person = 1;
COMMIT;
```

```
# Define a stored procedure
DELIMITER //
CREATE PROCEDURE person_counter (OUT pcount INT)
BEGIN
SELECT COUNT(*) INTO pcount FROM person;
END
//
DELIMITER ;
```

CALL

CALL procedure [([parameter [, …]])]

Calls the specified stored procedure with the named parameters.

Examples

```
CALL person_counter ( @pcount );
SELECT @pcount;
```

CHANGE MASTER

CHANGE MASTER TO param = value [, param = value] …

Changes the parameters a slave server uses to connect to a master during replication. You may specify any number of parameters. If a specific parameter is not specified, MySQL will use the current value for that parameter except MASTER_LOG_FILE and MASTER_LOG_POS. If those are not specified and new MASTER_HOST or MASTER_PORT values are specified, MySQL assumes you are referring to a new server (even if using the old values) and will thus use MySQL's default of '' and 4, respectively.

Available parameters include:

MASTER_CONNECT_RETRY
  The number of attempts a slave will make to connect to a master after a failure.

MASTER_HOST
  The IP address of the master server.

MASTER_LOG_FILE
  The name of the binary logfile on the master from which replication data is read.

MASTER_LOG_POS
> The transaction position specified via SHOW MASTER STATUS that helps the slave synchronize with the master.

MASTER_PASSWORD
> The password for the user on the master under which replication occurs.

MASTER_PORT
> If the master server is listening on a nonstandard port, this option enables you to specify what that port is.

MASTER_SSL
> Set to 1 if the master requires SSL, 0 otherwise.

MASTER_SSL_CA
> The CA file for SSL support.

MASTER_SSL_CA_PATH
> The directory where the CA file for SSL support is found.

MASTER_SSL_CERT
> The cert file for SSL support.

MASTER_SSL_CIPHER
> The cipher list in use for SSL support.

MASTER_SSL_KEY
> The name of the key file for SSL support.

MASTER_USER
> The name of the user on the master with REPLICATION SLAVE permissions enabled.

RELAY_LOG_FILE
> The logfile for the relay.

RELAY_LOG_POS
> The synchronization position in the relay log.

Example

```
CHANGE MASTER TO MASTER_LOG_FILE='crm114-bin.000044',
MASTR_LOG_POS=665,
MASTER_HOST='mydb.imaginary.com', MASTER_USER='slave',
MASTER_PASSWORD='replicate';
```

CLOSE

CLOSE *cursor_name*

Closes the named cursor, rendering it no longer accessible. Any cursor not closed by the end of the compound statement in which it was declared is automatically closed.

COMMIT

COMMIT [WORK] [AND [NO] CHAIN] [[NO] RELEASE]

Commits the current transaction. Chaining causes a new transaction to begin immediately after a successful commit. RELEASE/NO RELEASE indicates whether the current client should be disconnected after completion.

CREATE DATABASE

CREATE DATABASE [IF NOT EXISTS] *dbname* [*create_options*]

Creates a new database with the specified name. You must have the proper privileges to create the database. Running this command is the same as running the *mysqladmin create* utility.

Example

```
CREATE DATABASE Bank;
CREATE DATABASE statistics CHARACTER SET utf8;
```

CREATE EVENT

CREATE [DEFINER = { *user* | CURRENT_USER}] EVENT [IF NOT EXISTS] *name*
  ON SCHEDULE *schedule*
  [ON COMPLETION [NOT] PRESERVE]
  [ENABLE | DISABLE]
  [COMMENT '*comment*']
  DO statement

MySQL 5.1 only. Creates an event that will execute the specified SQL statement in accordance with the defined event schedule.

The ON SCHEDULE clause establishes the schedule on which the event will run. There are two ways in which the define the schedule:

AT timestamp [+ INTERVAL interval]

> This schedules a one-time event to run at the specified timestamp. You may specify a time in the future relative to the timestamp using the INTERVAL clause. For example, you can combine CURRENT_TIMESTAMP with an interval value to have the event execute one hour from now.

EVERY interval [STARTS timestamp] [ENDS timestamp]

> This schedules a repeating event that runs according to a regular interval, optionally starting and ending at defined times in the future.

With all time values, you may use the keyword CURRENT_TIMESTAMP to specify the current date and time. The interval clause follows the following syntax:

```
quantity { YEAR | QUARTER | MONTH | WEEK | DAY | HOUR |
MINUTE | SECOND |
YEAR_MONTH | DAY_HOUR | DAY_MINUTE | DAY_SECOND | HOUR_
MINUTE | HOUR_SECOND |
MINUTE_SECOND }
```

The SQL statement may be any valid SQL. You may also elect to execute compound statements using BEGIN/END blocks in the same way you define stored procedures.

MySQL stores the current SQL mode setting with the event. As a result, events execute in accordance with the SQL mode in place when the event was created—not when it is being executed.

Example

```
# Create an event to run every month
CREATE EVENT monthly_cleaner
ON SCHEDULE EVERY 1 MONTH
DO DELETE FROM page_view;

# Create an event to run one time, 1 hour from now
CREATE EVENT in_an_hour_cleaner
ON SCHEDULE AT CURRENT_TIMESTAMP + INTERVAL 1 HOUR
DO DELETE FROM page_view;
```

CREATE FUNCTION

```
CREATE    [DEFINER={user    |    CURRENT_USER}]    FUNCTION    sp_name
([params]) RETURNS type
    function_definition
CREATE [AGGREGATE] FUNCTION name RETURNS return_type SONAME
library
```

MySQL has two distinct function concepts. The first syntax creates a *stored function*. Stored functions are defined much like stored procedures, except you can call a stored function like you can any built-in function or library function as part of your query. A stored function takes any number of IN parameters and issue a return value. *Library functions*—more commonly referred to as *user-defined functions* (UDFs)—are custom extensions of MySQL in an external programming language. These functions can perform practically any operation, since they are designed and implemented by the user. The return value of the function can be STRING, for character data; REAL, for floating point numbers; or INTEGER, for integer numbers. MySQL will translate the return value of the C function to the indicated type. The library file that contains the function must be a standard shared library that MySQL can dynamically link into the server.

Example

```
CREATE FUNCTION multiply RETURNS REAL SONAME mymath.so
```

CREATE INDEX

```
CREATE    [UNIQUE|FULLTEXT|SPATIAL]    INDEX    name    ON    table
(column[(length)], ...)
```

The CREATE INDEX statement is provided for compatibility with other implementations of SQL. In older versions of SQL, this statement does nothing. As of 3.22, this statement is equivalent to the ALTER TABLE ADD INDEX statement. To perform the CREATE INDEX statement, you must have INDEX privileges for the table in question.

The UNIQUE keyword constrains the table to having only one row in which the index columns have a given value. If the index is multicolumn, individual column values may be repeated; the whole index must be unique.

The FULLTEXT keyword enables keyword searching on the indexed column or columns. You may have FULLTEXT indexes only on MyISAM tables and only for CHAR, VARCHAR, or TEXT columns. SPATIAL indexes are also only allowed for non-NULL columns in MyISAM tables.

You can create indexes that use only part of a column by providing a length modifier to the column being indexed.

Example

```
CREATE UNIQUE INDEX TransIDX ON Translation ( language,
locale, code );
# Index the first 6 characters of a confirmation code:
CREATE INDEX InvIDX ON Invitation ( code(6) );
```

CREATE PROCEDURE

```
CREATE [DEFINER = { user | CURRENT_USER }] PROCEDURE name
([ {IN | OUT | INOUT} parameter data_type [, …]])
[LANGUAGE SQL] [[NOT] DETERMINISTIC]
[{CONTAINS SQL | NO SQL | READS SQL DATA | MODIFIES SQL DATA}]
[SQL SECURITY { DEFINER | INVOKER}]
[COMMENT 'comment string']
procedure_body
```

Creates a new stored procedure in MySQL. To use this command, you must have CREATE ROUTINE permission. The procedure body can be a simple SQL statement or a series of statements bound by a BEGIN/END pair. For more on BEGIN/END, see the BEGIN command or the section on stored procedures.

CREATE TABLE

```
CREATE [TEMPORARY] TABLE [IF NOT EXISTS] table
(create_clause, ...)
[table_options]
[[IGNORE|REPLACE] select]
CREATE [TEMPORARY] TABLE [IF NOT EXISTS] table LIKE old_table
```

The CREATE TABLE statement defines the structure of a table within the database. This statement is how all MySQL tables are created.

If the TEMPORARY keyword is used, the table exists only as long as the current client connection exists, or until you explicitly drop the table.

The IF NOT EXISTS clause tells MySQL to create the table only if the table does not already exist. If the table does exist, nothing happens. If the table exists and IF NOT EXISTS and TEMPORARY are not specified, an error will occur. If TEMPORARY is specified and the table exists but IF NOT EXISTS is not specified, the existing table will simply be invisible to this client for the duration of the new temporary table's life.

The CREATE clause can either define the structure of a specific column or define a metastructure for the column. A CREATE clause that defines a column consists of the name of the new table followed by any number of field definitions. The syntax of a field definition is:

```
column type [NOT NULL | NULL] [DEFAULT value]
[AUTO_INCREMENT] [PRIMARY KEY] [reference]
```

The modifiers in this syntax are:

AUTO_INCREMENT
:   Indicates that the column should be automatically incremented using the current greatest value for that column. Only whole number columns may be auto-incremented.

DEFAULT value
:   This attribute assigns a default value to a field. If a row is inserted into the table without a value for this field, this value will be inserted. If a default is not defined, a null value is inserted, unless the field is defined as NOT NULL in which case MySQL picks a value based on the type of the field.

NOT NULL
:   This attribute guarantees that every entry in the column will have some non-NULL value. Attempting to insert a NULL value into a field defined with NOT NULL will generate an error.

NULL
:   This attribute specifies that the field is allowed to contain NULL values. This is the default if neither this nor the NOT NULL modifier is specified. Fields within an index cannot contain the NULL modifier if they are PRIMARY KEY or SPATIAL indexes. (The attribute will be ignored, without warning, if it does exist in such a field.)

PRIMARY KEY

This attribute automatically makes the field the primary key (see later) for the table. Only one primary key may exist for a table. Any field that is a primary key must also contain the NOT NULL modifier.

REFERENCES*table* [*(column, . . .)]* [MATCH FULL | MATCH PARTIAL] [ON DELETE *option*] [ON UPDATE *option*]

Creates a foreign key reference. Currently applies only to the InnoDB table type.

You may specify metastructure such as indexes and constraints via the following clauses:

FULLTEXT (column, ...)

Since MySQL 3.23.23, MySQL has supported full text indexing. The use and results of this search are described in the online MySQL reference manual. To create a full text index, use the FULLTEXT keyword:

```
CREATE TABLE Item ( itemid INT NOT NULL PRIMARY KEY,
        name VARCHAR(25) NOT NULL,
        description TEXT NOT NULL,
        FULLTEXT ( name, description )
);
```

INDEX *[name]* *(column, ...)*

Creates a regular index of all of the named columns (KEY and INDEX, in this context, are synonyms). Optionally, the index may be given a name. If no name is provided, a name is assigned based on the first column given and a trailing number, if necessary, for uniqueness. If a key contains more than one column, leftmost subsets of those columns are also included in the index. Consider the following index definition:

```
INDEX idx1 ( name, rank, serial );
```

When this index is created, the following groups of columns will be indexed:

- name, rank, serial
- name, rank
- name

KEY *[name]* *(column, ...)*
    Synonym for INDEX.

PRIMARY KEY
    Creates the primary key of the table. A primary key is a special key that can be defined only once in a table. The primary key is a UNIQUE key with the name PRIMARY. Despite its privileged status, it behaves almost the same as every other unique key, except it does not allow NULL values.

UNIQUE *[name]* *(column, ...)*
    Creates a special index where every value contained in the index except NULL values (and therefore in the fields indexed) must be unique. Attempting to insert a value that already exists into a unique index will generate an error. The following would create a unique index of the nicknames field:

```
UNIQUE (nicknames);
```

When indexing character fields (CHAR, VARCHAR, and their synonyms only), it is possible to index only a prefix of the entire field. For example, the following will create an index of the numeric field id along with the first 20 characters of the character field address:

```
INDEX adds ( id, address(20) );
```

BLOB and TEXT columns require a prefix.

When performing any searches of the field address, only the first 20 characters will be used for comparison, unless more than one match is found that contains the same first 20 characters, in which case a regular search of the data is performed. Therefore, it can be a big performance bonus to index only the number of characters in a text field that you know will make the value unique. This feature is, however, dependent on the underlying table type.

In addition, MySQL supports the following special "types," and the MySQL team is working on adding functionality to support them:

```
FOREIGN KEY (name (column, [column2, . . . ])
CHECK
```

As of MySQL 3.23, you can specify table options at the end of a CREATE TABLE statement. These options are:

AUTO_INCREMENT = start
    Specifies the first value to be used for an AUTO_INCREMENT column. Works with MyISAM, InnoDB, and MEMORY tables.

AVG_ROW_LENGTH = length
    An option for tables containing large amounts of variable-length data. The average row length is an optimization hint to help MySQL manage this data.

CHECKSUM = 0 or 1
    When set to 1, this option forces MySQL to maintain a checksum for the table to improve data consistency. This option creates a performance penalty.

COMMENT = comment
    Provides a comment for the table. The comment may not exceed 60 characters.

DELAY_KEY_WRITE = 0 or 1
    For MyISAM tables only. When set, this option delays key table updates until the table is closed.

ENGINE = engine
    Specifies the table type of the database. If the selected table type is not available, the closest table type available is used. For example, BDB is not available for Mac OS X. If you specified TYPE=BDB on a Mac OS X system, MySQL will instead create the table as a MyISAM table (the default table type). Supported table types are described later.

MAX_ROWS = rowcount
    The maximum number of rows you intend to store in the table.

MIN_ROWS = rowcount
    The minimum number of rows you intend to store in the table.

PACK_KEYS = 0 or 1
    For MyISAM tables only. This option provides a performance booster for read-heavy tables. Set to 1, this option causes smaller keys to be created and thus slows down writes while speeding up reads.

PASSWORD = *'password'*

Available only to MySQL customers with special commercial licenses. This option uses the specified password to encrypt the table's *.frm* file. This option has no effect on the standard version of MySQL.

ROW_FORMAT = DYNAMIC or STATIC (MyISAM) COMPACT or REDUNDANT (InnoDB)

Defines how the rows should be stored in a table.

Finally, you can create a table and populate it straight from the results of a SQL query:

```
CREATE TABLE tblname SELECT query
```

You must have CREATE privileges on a database to use the CREATE TABLE statement.

Examples

```
# Create the new empty database 'employees'
CREATE DATABASE employees;
# Create a simple table
CREATE TABLE emp_data ( id INT, name CHAR(50) );
# Create a complex table
CREATE TABLE IF NOT EXISTS emp_review (
  id INT NOT NULL PRIMARY KEY AUTO_INCREMENT,
  emp_id INT NOT NULL REFERENCES emp_data ( id ),
  review TEXT NOT NULL,
  INDEX ( emp_id ),
  FULLTEXT ( review )
) AUTO_INCREMENT = 1, ENGINE=MyISAM;
# Make the function make_coffee (which returns a string
# value and is stored in the myfuncs.so shared library)
# available to MySQL.
CREATE FUNCTION make_coffee RETURNS string SONAME
"myfuncs.so";
# Create a table using the resultss from another query
CREATE TABLE Stadium
SELECT stadiumName, stadiumLocation
FROM City;
```

CREATE TABLESPACE

```
CREATE TABLESPACE tablespace
  ADD DATAFILE 'file'
  USE LOGFILE GROUP logfile_group
  [EXTENT SIZE = extent_size]
  [INITIAL SIZE = initial_size]
  ENGINE = engine
```

Creates a tablespace on the file system to support the storage of database tables. You can later add additional data files through the ALTER TABLESPACE command. In MySQL 5.1, the ENGINE parameter must be either NDB or NDBCLUSTER.

CREATE TRIGGER

```
CREATE [DEFINER = { user | CURRENT_USER }]
  TRIGGER trigger _name trigger_time trigger_event
  ON table FOR EACH ROW statement
```

Creates a trigger in MySQL. You may define at most one trigger per table/time/event. For example, you may define a trigger to run on BEFORE any INSERT into the person table and another to run AFTER an INSERT into the person table. You cannot, however, define multiple triggers to run BEFORE an INSERT into the person table. When activated, the trigger runs under the privileges specified in the DEFINER clause.

The trigger time defines whether the trigger should run BEFORE or AFTER the event in question. The event may be triggered by an INSERT, UPDATE, or DELETE.

Examples

```
# Make sure all addresses for a person are deleted when
the person is deleted
CREATE TRIGGER zap_addresses after DELETE ON person
FOR EACH ROW
BEGIN
  DELETE FROM address WHERE person = OLD.person_id;
END
```

CREATE USER

```
CREATE USER user
 [IDENTIFIED BY [PASSWORD] 'password']
 [, user [IDENTIFIED BY [PASSWORD] 'password']] ...
```

Creates a new user in MySQL.

CREATE VIEW

```
CREATE  [OR  REPLACE]  [ALGORITHM  =  {UNDEFINED  |  MERGE  |
TEMPTABLE}]
 [DEFINER = { user | CURRENT_USER }]
 [SQL SECURITY { DEFINER | INVOKER }]
 VIEW name [(columns)]
 AS select_statement
 [WITH [CASCADED | LOCAL] CHECK OPTION]
```

Creates a new view in MySQL based on the specified SQL query
and options. If the view already exists and OR REPLACE is specified,
the view will be replaced with the new data. Views and tables
share the same namespace, so you cannot create a view that shares
the same name as a table in the system (and vice versa).

The default names for the view's columns are the names from the
select. Because the view column names must be unique, it generally makes sense to provide custom names. If you do so, the list of
column names must match the number of columns in your SELECT
statement.

Examples

```
CREATE VIEW person_view
AS
SELECT first_name, last_name, email_type, email_address
FROM person, address
WHERE person.person_id = email_address.person
```

DECLARE

```
DECLARE name [,...] sql_type [DEFAULT value]
DECLARE name CURSOR FOR statement
DECLARE condition CONDITION
 FOR {SQLSTATE [VALUE] sqlstate | mysql_error_code}
DECLARE {CONTINUE | EXIT | UNDO} HANDLER
 FOR {condition | SQLSTATE [VALUE] sqlstate | mysql_error_code
 | SQLWARNING | NOTFOUND | SQLEXCEPTION } statement
```

The first syntax defines local variables for stored procedure definitions.

The second syntax enables you to declare a cursor to use in a stored procedure.

The third and fourth syntaxes define condition handlers for specific conditions. The third syntax created a named condition that references either a specific SQL state code or a MySQL error code. The fourth syntax lets you define a handler to process specified conditions either based on a name you previously defined or using other condition definitions.

DELIMITER

```
DELIMITER delimiter
```

Alters the delimiter used to end SQL statements in MySQL. The default delimiter is the semicolon (;). The most common instance in which you would want to change the delimiter is when defining a stored procedure. When changing the delimiter, avoid using the backspace (\) character as it has special meaning in MySQL.

Examples

```
DELIMITER //
```

DELETE

```
DELETE [LOW_PRIORITY | QUICK]
 FROM table
 [WHERE clause]
 [ORDER BY column, ...] [LIMIT n]
DELETE [LOW_PRIORITY | QUICK] table1[.*], table2[.*], ...,
tablen[.*]
 FROM tablex, tabley, ..., tablez
 [WHERE clause]
DELETE [LOW_PRIORITY | QUICK]
 FROM table1[.*], table2[.*], ..., tablen[.*]
 USING references
 [WHERE clause]
```

Deletes rows from a table. When used without a WHERE clause, this erases the entire table and recreates it as an empty table. With a WHERE clause, it deletes the rows that match the condition of the clause. This statement returns the number of rows deleted.

In versions prior to MySQL 4, omitting the WHERE clause erases this entire table. This is done by using an efficient method that is much faster than deleting each row individually. When using this method, MySQL returns 0 to the user because it has no way of knowing how many rows it deleted. In the current design, this method simply deletes all the files associated with the table except for the file that contains the actual table definition. Therefore, this is a handy method of zeroing out tables with unrecoverable corrupt data files. You will lose the data, but the table structure will still be in place. If you really wish to get a full count of all deleted rows, use a WHERE clause with an expression that always evaluates to true:

```
DELETE FROM TBL WHERE 1 = 1;
```

The LOW_PRIORITY modifier causes MySQL to wait until no clients are reading from the table before executing the delete. For MyISAM tables, QUICK causes the table handler to suspend the merging of indexes during the DELETE, to enhance the speed of the DELETE.

The LIMIT clause establishes the maximum number of rows that will be deleted in a single execution.

When deleting from MyISAM tables, MySQL simply deletes references in a linked list to the space formerly occupied by the deleted rows. The space itself is not returned to the operating system. Future inserts will eventually occupy the deleted space. If, however, you need the space immediately, run the OPTIMIZE TABLE statement or use the *mysqlcheck* utility.

The second two syntaxes are multitable DELETE statements that enable the deletion of rows from multiple tables. The first is available as of MySQL 4.0.0, and the second was introduced in MySQL 4.0.2.

In the first multitable DELETE syntax, the FROM clause does not name the tables from which the DELETEs occur. Instead, the objects of the DELETE command are the tables from which the deletes should occur. The FROM clause in this syntax works like a FROM clause in a SELECT in that it names all of the tables that appear either as objects of the DELETE or in the WHERE clause.

I recommend the second multitable DELETE syntax because it avoids confusion with the single table DELETE. In other words, it deletes rows from the tables specified in the FROM clause. The USING clause describes all the referenced tables in the FROM and WHERE clauses. The following two DELETEs do the exact same thing. Specifically, they delete all records from the emp_data and emp_review tables for employees in a specific department.

```
DELETE emp_data, emp_review
FROM emp_data, emp_review, dept
WHERE dept.id = emp_data.dept_id
AND emp_data.id = emp_review.emp_id
AND dept.id = 32;
DELETE FROM emp_data, emp_review
USING emp_data, emp_review, dept
WHERE dept.id = emp_data.dept_id
AND emp_data.id = emp_review.emp_id
AND dept.id = 32;
```

You must have DELETE privileges on a database to use the DELETE statement.

Examples

```
# Erase all of the data (but not the table itself)
for the table 'olddata'.
DELETE FROM olddata
# Erase all records in the 'sales' table where the 'syear'
field is '1995'.
DELETE FROM sales WHERE syear=1995
```

DESCRIBE

```
DESCRIBE table [column]
DESC table [column]
```

Gives information about a table or column. While this statement works as advertised, its functionality is available (along with much more) in the SHOW statement. This statement is included solely for compatibility with Oracle SQL. The optional column name can contain SQL wildcards, in which case information will be displayed for all matching columns.

Example

```
# Describe the layout of the table 'messy'
DESCRIBE messy
# Show the information about any columns starting
# with 'my_' in the 'big' table.
# Remember: '_' is a wildcard, too, so it must be
# escaped to be used literally.
DESC big my\_%
```

DESC

Synonym for DESCRIBE.

DO

```
DO expression [, expression, ...]
```

Executes expressions without returning any results.

DROP DATABASE

DROP DATABASE [IF EXISTS] *name*

Permanently remove a database from MySQL. Once you execute this statement, none of the tables or data that made up the database are available. All support files for the database are deleted from the filesystem. The number of files deleted will be returned to the user. This statement is equivalent to running the *mysqladmin drop* utility. As with running *mysqladmin*, you must be the administrative user for MySQL (usually root or mysql) to perform this statement. You may use the IF EXISTS clause to prevent any error message that would result from an attempt to drop a nonexistent database.

DROP EVENT

DROP EVENT [IF EXISTS] *name*

Drops the specified event from MySQL. You must have the EVENT privilege to be able to drop an event.

DROP FUNCTION

DROP FUNCTION [IF EXISTS] *name*

Will remove a user-defined or stored function from the running MySQL server process. This does not actually delete the library file containing the function. You may add the function again at any time using the CREATE FUNCTION statement. In the current implementation, DROP FUNCTION simply removes the function from the function table within the MySQL database. This table keeps track of all active functions.

DROP INDEX

DROP INDEX *idx_name* ON *tbl_name*

Provides compatibility with other SQL implementations. In older versions of MySQL, this statement does nothing. As of 3.22, this statement is equivalent to ALTER TABLE ... DROP INDEX. To perform the DROP INDEX statement, you must have SELECT, INSERT, DELETE, UPDATE, CREATE, and DROP privileges for the table in question.

DROP PROCEDURE

DROP PROCEDURE [IF EXISTS] *name*

Removes the specified procedure from the database. You must have ALTER ROUTINE permissions for the procedure in order to execute this call.

DROP TABLE

DROP TABLE [IF EXISTS] *name* [, *name2*, ...] [RESTRICT | CASCADE]

Will erase an entire table permanently. In the current implementation, MySQL simply deletes the files associated with the table. As of 3.22, you may specify IF EXISTS to make MySQL not return an error if you attempt to remove a table that does not exist. The RESTRICT and CASCADE keywords do nothing; they exist solely for ANSI compatibility. You must have DELETE privileges on the table to use this statement.

DROP TABLESPACE

DROP TABLESPACE *tablespace* ENGINE = *engine*

Drops the specified tablespace. The tablespace must not include any data files. You should therefore make sure you remove all data files first by using the ALTER TABLESPACE command.

DROP TRIGGER

DROP TRIGGER [IF EXISTS] *trigger*

Drops the specified trigger from MySQL. When upgrading from MySQL 5.0.10 and earlier to any later version, you must first drop your triggers before the upgrade and then re-add them.

DROP USER

DROP USER *user*

Drops a user from MySQL along with his permissions.

DROP VIEW

```
DROP VIEW [IF EXISTS] view [RESTRICT | CASCADE]
```

Drops the specified view from the system. The RESTRICT and CASCADE options are ignored in MySQL.

EXPLAIN

```
EXPLAIN table_name
EXPLAIN [EXTENDED] query
```

Used with a table name, this command is an alias for SHOW COLUMNS FROM table_name.

Used with an SQL statement, this command displays verbose information about the order and structure of a SELECT statement. This can be used to see where keys are not being used efficiently. This information is returned as a result set with the following columns:

table

> The name of the table referenced by the result set row explaining the query.

type

> The type of join that will be performed.

possible_keys

> Indicates which indexes MySQL could use to build the join. If this column is empty, there are no relevant indexes and you should probably build some to enhance performance.

key

> Indicates which index MySQL decided to use.

key_len

> Provides the length of the key MySQL decided to use for the join.

ref

> Describes which columns or constants were used with the key to build the join.

rows

> Indicates the number of rows MySQL estimates it will need to examine to perform the query.

Extra

Additional information indicating how MySQL will perform the query.

Example

```
EXPLAIN SELECT customer.name, product.name FROM customer,
product, purchases
WHERE purchases.customer=customer.id AND purchases.
product=product.id
```

FETCH

```
FETCH cursor_name INTO var [,...]
```

Fetches the next row of data from an open cursor and advances the cursor one row. To detect when no more rows are available, you need to set up a handler to catch SQL state 02000 (NO DATA).

FLUSH

```
FLUSH option[, option...]
```

Flushes or resets various internal processes depending on the options given. You must have RELOAD privileges to execute this statement. The option can be any of the following:

DES_KEY_FILE

Reloads the DES keys from the file originally specified with the --des-key-file option.

HOSTS

Empties the cache table that stores hostname information for clients. This should be used if a client changes IP addresses, or if there are errors related to connecting to the host.

LOGS

Closes all the logfiles and reopens them. This can be used if a logfile has changed its inode number. If no specific extension has been given to the binary log, a new binary log will be opened with the extension incremented by one.

PRIVILEGES

Reloads all the internal MySQL permissions grant tables. This must be run for any changes to the tables to take effect unless those changes occurred through a GRANT/REVOKE statement.

QUERY CACHE
> Defragments the query cache to improve memory use, but it does not delete queries from the cache.

STATUS
> Resets the status variables that keep track of the current state of the server.

TABLE *table*

TABLES *table, table2, ..., tablen*
> Flushes only the specified tables.

TABLES [WITH READ LOCK]
> Closes all currently open tables and flushes any cached data to disk. With a read lock, it acquires a read lock that will not be released until UNLOCK TABLES is issued

---

GRANT

```
GRANT privilege [ (column, ...) ] [, privilege [( column, ...) ]
...]
ON [{TABLE | FUNCTION | PROCEDURE}] {table
| * | *.* | database.*}
TO user [IDENTIFIED BY 'password'] [, user [IDENTIFIED BY
'password'] ...]
[REQUIRE [{NONE | SSL | X509 | CIPHER cipher [AND] [ISSUER
issuer [AND]]
[SUBJECT subject]]]]
[WITH [GRANT OPTION]
[MAX_QUERIES_PER_HOUR limit]
 [MAX_UPDATES_PER_HOUR limit]
 [MAX_CONNECTIONS_PER_HOUR limit]
 [MAX_USER_CONNECTIONS limit]]
```

In versions prior to MySQL 3.22.11, the GRANT statement was recognized but did nothing. In current versions, GRANT is functional. This statement enables access rights to a user (or users). Access can be granted per database, table or individual column. The table can be given as a table within the current database; use * to affect all tables within the current database, *.* to affect all tables within all databases, or database.* to affect all tables within the given database.

The following privileges are currently supported:

ALL PRIVILEGES/ALL

Assigns all privileges available to the user under which you are performing this GRANT except FILE, PROCESS, RELOAD, and SHUTDOWN.

ALTER

To alter the structure of tables.

ALTER ROUTINE

To make changes to a stored procedure or function.

CREATE

To create new tables.

CREATE ROUTINE

To create a stored procedure or function.

CREATE TEMPORARY TABLES

To create temporary tables.

CREATE USER

To create new users.

CREATE VIEW

To create views.

DELETE

To delete rows from tables.

DROP

To delete entire tables.

EVENT

To create scheduler events.

EXECUTE

To execute stored procedures and functions.

FILE

To create and remove entire databases, as well as manage logfiles.

GRANT OPTION

To grant privileges to other users.

INDEX

To create and delete indexes from tables.

INSERT

To insert data into tables.

LOCK TABLES
> To issue LOCK TABLES on tables for which you have a SELECT privilege.

PROCESS
> To view process threads.

REFERENCES
> Not implemented (yet).

RELOAD
> To refresh various internal tables (see the FLUSH statement).

REPLICATION CLIENT
> To ask where slave and master servers are.

REPLICATION SLAVE
> To enable a slave to read events from the master binary logfile.

SELECT
> To read data from tables.

SHOW DATABASES
> To see all databases on the server.

SHOW VIEW
> To execute SHOW CREATE VIEW.

SHUTDOWN
> To shut down the database server.

SUPER
> To execute a variety of administrative commands and to bypass max_connections.

TRIGGER
> To create or drop triggers.

UPDATE
> To alter rows within tables.

USAGE
> No privileges at all.

The user variable is of the form *user@hostname*. Either the user or the hostname can contain SQL wildcards. When wildcards are used, either the whole name must be quoted, or just the parts with the wildcards (e.g., joe@"%.com " and "joe@%.com" are both valid). A user without a hostname is considered to be the same as user@"%".

If you have a global GRANT privilege, you may specify an optional INDENTIFIED BY modifier. If the user in the statement does not exist, it will be created with the given password. Otherwise, the existing user will have her password changed.

The GRANT privilege is given to a user with the WITH GRANT OPTION modifier. If this is used, the user may grant any privilege she has to another user. You may also chose to limit the number of queries made by a particular user ID through the MAX_QUERIES_PER_HOUR option.

Support for secure SSL encryptions, as well as X.509 authentication, exists in MySQL. The REQUIRE clause enables you to require a user to authenticate in one of these manners and identify the credentials to be used. Just specifying REQUIRE SSL tells MySQL that the user can connect to MySQL using only an SSL connection. Similarly, REQUIRE X509 requires the user to authenticate using an X.509 certificate. You can place the following restrictions on the connection:

ISSUER *issuer*
> Demands that the certificate have the issuer specified.

SUBJECT *subject*
> Not only does the user have to have a valid certificate, but it must have a certificate for the specified subject.

CIPHER *cipher*
> Enables MySQL to enforce a minimum encryption strength. The connection must use one of the ciphers specified here.

Examples

```
# Give full access to joe@carthage for the Account table
GRANT ALL ON bankdb.Account TO joe@carthage;
# Give full access to jane@carthage for the
# Account table and create a user ID/password for her
GRANT ALL ON bankdb.Account TO jane@carthage IDENTIFIED BY
'mypass';
# Give joe the ability
# to SELECT from any table on the webdb database
GRANT SELECT ON webdb.* TO joe;
```

---

* In fact, the rules governing when you need to use quotes are more complex. As a good rule of thumb, whenever you have nonalphanumeric characters, quote them.

```
# Give joe on the local machine access to everything in
webdb but
# require some special security
GRANT ALL on webdb.* TO joe@localhost
IDENTIFIED BY 'mypass'
REQUIRE SUBJECT 'C=US, ST=MN, L=Minneapolis, O=My Cert,
CN=Joe Friday/Email=joe@localhost'
AND ISSUER='C=US, ST=MN, L=Minneapolis, O=Imaginet,
CN=Joe Friday/Email=joe@localhost'
AND CIPHER='RSA-DES-3DES-SHA';
```

INSERT

```
INSERT [DELAYED | LOW_PRIORITY ] [IGNORE]
 [INTO] table [ (column, ...) ]
 VALUES ( values [, values... ])
 [ ON DUPLICATE KEY UPDATE col=expression ]
INSERT [DELAYED | LOW_PRIORITY] [IGNORE]
 [INTO] table [ (column, ...) ]
 SELECT ...
[ ON DUPLICATE KEY UPDATE col=expression ]
INSERT [DELAYED | LOW_PRIORITY] [IGNORE]
 [INTO] table
 SET column=value, column=value,...
[ ON DUPLICATE KEY UPDATE col=expression ]
```

Inserts data into a table. The first form of this statement simply
inserts the given values into the given columns. Columns in the
table that are not given values are set to their default values or
NULL. The second form takes the results of a SELECT query and
inserts them into the table. The third form is simply an alternate
version of the first form that more explicitly shows which columns
correspond with which values. If the DELAYED modifier is present in
the first form, all incoming SELECT statements will be given
priority over the insert, which will wait until the other activity has
finished before inserting the data. In a similar way, using the LOW_
PRIORITY modifier with any form of INSERT causes the insertion to
be postponed until all other operations from other clients have
been finished.

Starting with MySQL 3.22.5, it is possible to insert more than one row into a table at a time. This is done by adding additional value lists to the statement separated by commas.

If ON DUPLICATE KEY UPDATED is used, an UPDATE is performed on the existing row when an INSERT would duplicate that row due to a key match.

You must have INSERT privileges to use this statement.

Examples

```
# Insert a record into the 'people' table.
INSERT INTO people ( name, rank, serial_number )
VALUES ( 'Bob Smith', 'Captain', 12345 );
# Copy all records from 'data' that are older than a
certain date into
# 'old_data'. This would usually be followed by deleting
the old data from
# 'data'.
INSERT INTO old_data ( id, date, field )
SELECT ( id, date, field)
FROM data
WHERE date < 87459300;
# Insert 3 new records into the 'people' table.
INSERT INTO people (name, rank, serial_number )
VALUES ( 'Tim O''Reilly', 'General', 1),
  ('Andy Oram', 'Major', 4342),
  ('Randy Yarger', 'Private', 9943);
# Update on duplicate key
INSERT INTO people ( person_id, first_name, last_name )
VALUES ( 1, 'George', 'Reese' )
ON DUPLICATE KEY UPDATE people SET person_id = person_id +
1 WHERE person_id = 1;
```

KILL

KILL [CONNECTION | QUERY] *thread_id*

KILL CONNECTION is the same as KILL with no modifier.

Terminates the specified thread. The thread ID numbers can be found using SHOW PROCESSLIST. Killing threads owned by users other than yourself requires PROCESS privilege. In MySQL 4.x, this privilege is now the SUPER privilege.

Example

```
# Terminate thread 3
KILL 3
```

LOAD

```
LOAD DATA [LOW_PRIORITY | CONCURRENT] [LOCAL] INFILE file
[REPLACE|IGNORE]
  INTO TABLE table [delimiters] [(columns)]
```

Reads a text file and inserts its data into a database table. This method of inserting data is much quicker than using multiple INSERT statements. Although the statement may be sent from all clients like any other SQL statement, the file referred to in the statement is assumed to be located on the server unless the LOCAL keyword is used. If the filename does not have a fully qualified path, MySQL looks under the directory of the current database for the file.

With no delimiters specified, LOAD DATA INFILE will assume that the file is tab delimited with character fields, special characters escaped with backslashes (\), and lines terminated with newline characters.

In addition to the default behavior, you may specify your own delimiters using the following keywords. Delimiters apply to all tables in the statement.

FIELDS TERMINATED BY 'c'
> Specifies the character used to delimit the fields. The escape codes listed earlier in the section on literals can be used to designate special characters. This value may contain more than one character. For example, FIELDS TERMINATED BY "," denotes a comma-delimited file and FIELDS TERMINATED BY "\t" denotes tab delimited. The default value is tab delimited.

FIELDS ENCLOSED BY 'c'
> Specifies the character used to enclose character strings. For example, FIELD ENCLOSED BY "'" would mean that a line containing "one, two", "other", "last" would be taken to have three fields:
> - one, two
> - other
> - last

The default behavior is to assume that no quoting is used in the file.

FIELDS ESCAPED BY 'c'

Specifies the character used to indicate that the next character is not special, even though it would usually be a special character. For example, with FIELDS ESCAPED BY '^' a line consisting of First,Second^,Third,Fourth would be parsed as three fields: "First", "Second,Third", and "Fourth". The exceptions to this rule are the null characters. Assuming the FIELDS ESCAPED BY value is a backslash, \0 indicates an ASCII NUL (character number 0) and \N indicates a MySQL NULL value. The default value is the backslash character. Note that MySQL itself considers the backslash character to be special. Therefore, to indicate backslash in that statement, you must backslash the backslash like this: FIELDS ESCAPED BY '\\'.

LINES TERMINATED BY 'c'

Specifies the character that indicates the end of a new record. This value can contain more than one character. For example, with LINES TERMINATED BY '.', a file consisting of a,b,c. d,e,f.g,h,k would be parsed as three separate records, each containing three fields. The default is the newline character. This means that by default, MySQL assumes each line is a separate record.

IGNORE number LINES

Ignores the specified number of lines before it loads.

By default, if a value read from the file is the same as an existing value in the table for a field that is part of a unique key, an error is given. If the REPLACE keyword is added to the statement, the entire row from the table will be replaced with values from the file. Conversely, the IGNORE keyword causes MySQL to ignore the new value and keep the old one.

The word NULL encountered in the data file is considered to indicate a null value unless the FIELDS ENCLOSED BY character encloses it, or if no FIELDS ENCLOSED BY clause is specified.

Using the same character for more than one delimiter can confuse MySQL. For example, FIELDS TERMINATED BY ',' ENCLOSED BY ',' would produce unpredictable behavior.

If a list of columns is provided, the data is inserted into those particular fields in the table. If no columns are provided, and the fields must be in the same order as the fields are defined in the table. Extra fields are ignored, and any missing fields are assigned default values.

You must have SELECT and INSERT privileges on the table to use this statement.

Example

```
# Load in the data contained in 'mydata.txt' into the
# table 'mydata'. Assume
# that the file is tab delimited with no quotes
# surrounding the fields.
LOAD DATA INFILE 'mydata.txt' INTO TABLE mydata
# Load in the data contained in 'newdata.txt' Look for two
# comma delimited
# fields and insert their values into the fields 'field1'
# and 'field2' in
# the 'newtable' table.
LOAD DATA INFILE 'newdata.txt'
INTO TABLE newtable
FIELDS TERMINATED BY ','
( field1, field2 )
```

LOCK

```
LOCK TABLES name
 [AS alias] {READ | [READ LOCAL] | [LOW_PRIORITY] WRITE}
 [, name2 [AS alias] {READ | [READ LOCAL] | LOW_PRIORITY]
WRITE, ...]
```

Locks a table for the use of a specific thread. This command is generally used to emulate transactions. If a thread creates a READ lock, all other threads may read from the table, but only the controlling thread can write to the table. If a thread creates a WRITE lock, no other thread may read from or write to the table.

Example

```
# Lock tables 'table1' and 'table3' to prevent updates,
and block all access
# to 'table2'. Also create the alias 't3' for 'table3' in
the current thread.
LOCK TABLES table1 READ, table2 WRITE, table3 AS t3 READ
```

OPEN

```
OPEN cursor_name
```

Opens the previously declared cursor specified in the statement.

OPTIMIZE

```
OPTIMIZE TABLE name
```

Recreates a table, eliminating any wasted space and sorting any unsorted index pages. Also updates any statistics that are not currently up to date. This task is performed by creating the optimized table as a separate, temporary table and using it to replace the current table. This command currently works only for MyISAM, InnoDB, and ARCHIVE tables. If you want the syntax to work no matter what table type you use, you should run *mysqld* with `--skip-new` or `--safe-mode` on. Under these circumstances, `OPTIMIZE TABLE` is an alias for `ALTER TABLE`.

Example

```
OPTIMIZE TABLE mytable
```

RELEASE SAVEPOINT

```
RELEASE SAVEPOINT savepoint
```

Deletes the specified save point.

RENAME DATABASE

```
RENAME DATABASE original_name TO new_name
```

Renames the specified database. You must go back and manually alter any permissions granted under the old name as they will not be automatically converted to the new name.

`RENAME SCHEMA` is a synonym for this command.

RENAME USER

```
RENAME USER original_name TO new_name
```

Renames the specified user. If you specify only the name part of the user, '%' will be added for the host name part.

REPLACE

```
REPLACE [DELAYED | LOW_PRIORITY] INTO table [(column, ...)]
VALUES (value, ...) REPLACE [DELAYED | LOW_PRIORITY] INTO table
[(column, ...)] SELECT select_clause REPLACE [DELAYED | LOW_
PRIORITY] INTO table SET column=value, column=value, ...
```

Inserts data into a table, replacing any old data that conflicts. This statement is identical to INSERT except that if a value conflicts with an existing unique key, the new value replaces the old one. The first form of this statement simply inserts the given values into the given columns. Columns in the table that are not given values are set to their default values or to NULL. The second form takes the results of a SELECT query and inserts them into the table. The final form inserts specific values using a syntax similar to an UPDATE statement, but it always replaces the entire row—not just the specified values.

Examples

```
# Insert a record into the 'people' table.
REPLACE INTO people ( name, rank, serial_number )
VALUES ( 'Bob Smith', 'Captain', 12345 )
# Copy all records from 'data' that are older than a
certain date into
# 'old_data'. This would usually be followed by deleting
the old data from
# 'data'.
REPLACE INTO old_data ( id, date, field )
SELECT ( id, date, field)
FROM data
WHERE date < 87459300
```

REVOKE

```
REVOKE privilege [(column, ...)] [, privilege [(column, ...) ...]
ON table
FROM user
REVOKE ALL PRIVILEGES, GRANT OPTION FROM user [, user ...]
```

Removes a privilege from a user. The values of privilege, table, and user are the same as for the GRANT statement. You must have the GRANT privilege to be able to execute this statement. See the GRANT statement for more details.

ROLLBACK

```
ROLLBACK [WORK] [AND [NO] CHAIN] [[NO] RELEASE] [TO SAVEPOINT
savepoint]
```

Rolls back the current transaction, undoing any work since the most recent BEGIN (or, if chaining is in use, since the last COMMIT or ROLLBACK). If a save point is specified, the transaction is moved back to the identified save point. Any save points after the specified save point are deleted.

SAVEPOINT

```
SAVEPOINT savepoint
```

Defines a save point for a transaction. You can later use the ROLLBACK TO SAVEPOINT syntax of the ROLLBACK command to roll the transaction back to the point identified by this save point.

SELECT

```
SELECT
  [STRAIGHT_JOIN] [SQL_SMALL_RESULT] [SQL_BIG_RESULT]
  [SQL_BUFFER_RESULT] [SQL_CACHE | SQL_NO_CACHE]
  [SQL_CALC_FOUND_ROWS] [HIGH_PRIORITY] [DISTINCT | |
  DISTINCTROW | ALL]
   column [[AS] alias][, ...]
  [INTO {OUTFILE 'filename' delimiters | DUMPFILE 'filename' |
  @variable}]
  [FROM table [[AS] alias]
  [WHERE condition [, ...]]
  [GROUP BY {column | expression | position} [ASC | DESC] [, ...]
  [WITH ROLLUP]]
  [HAVING condition]
  [ORDER BY {column | expression | position} [ASC | DESC] [, ...] ]
  [LIMIT {offset | row_limit | row_limit OFFSET offset}]
  [PROCEDURE name (arg [, ...])]
  [FOR UPDATE | LOCK IN SHARE MODE]
  [UNION [ALL] select substatement]
```

Retrieves data from a database. The SELECT statement is the primary method of reading data from database tables.

If the DISTINCT keyword is present, only one row of data will be output for every group of rows that is identical. The ALL keyword is the opposite of DISTINCT and displays all returned data. The default behavior is ALL. DISTINCT and DISTINCTROWS are synonyms.

MySQL provides several extensions to the basic ANSI SQL syntax that help modify how your query runs:

HIGH_PRIORITY
    Increases the priority with which the query is run, even to the extent of ignoring tables waiting to be locked for update. You can cause database updates to grind to a halt if you use this option with long-running queries.

STRAIGHT_JOIN
    If you specify more than one table, MySQL will automatically join the tables so that you can compare values between them. In cases where MySQL does not perform the join in an efficient manner, you can specify STRAIGHT_JOIN to force MySQL to join the tables in the order you enter them in the query.

SQL_BUFFER_RESULT
    Forces MySQL to store the result in a temporary table.

SQL_CALC_FOUND_ROWS
    Enables you to find out how many rows the query would return without a LIMIT clause. You can retrieve this value using SELECT FOUND_ROWS( ).

SQL_BIG_RESULT

SQL_SMALL_RESULT
    Both clauses tell MySQL what size you think the result set will be for use with GROUP BY or DISTINCT. With small results, MySQL will place the results in fast temporary tables instead of using sorting. Big results, however, will be placed in disk-based temporary tables and use sorting.

SQL_CACHE

SQL_NO_CACHE
    SQL_NO_CACHE dictates that MySQL should not store the query results in a query cache. SQL_CACHE, on the other hand, indicates that the results should be stored in a query cache if you are using cache on demand (SQL_QUERY_CACHE_TYPE=2).

The selected columns' values can be any one of the following:

Aliases

Any complex column name or function can be simplified by creating an alias for it. The value can be referred to by its alias anywhere else in the SELECT statement (e.g., SELECT DATE_ FORMAT(date,"%W, %M %d %Y") as nice_date FROM calendar). You cannot use aliases in WHERE clauses, as their values are not be calculated at that point.

Column names

These can be specified as column, table.column or database. table.column. The longer forms are necessary only to disambiguate columns with the same name, but can be used at any time (e.g., SELECT name FROM people; SELECT mydata.people. name FROM people).

Functions

MySQL supports a wide range of built-in functions such as SELECT COS(angle) FROM triangle (see later). In addition, user-defined functions can be added at any time using the CREATE FUNCTION statement.

By default, MySQL sends all output to the client that sent the query. It is possible however, to have the output redirected to a file. In this way you can dump the contents of a table (or selected parts of it) to a formatted file that can either be human readable, or formatted for easy parsing by another database system.

The INTO OUTFILE 'filename' modifier is the means in which output redirection is accomplished. With this, the results of the SELECT query are put into *filename*. The format of the file is determined by the delimiters arguments, which are the same as the LOAD DATA INFILE statement with the following additions:

- The OPTIONALLY keyword may be added to the FIELDS ENCLOSED BY modifier. This causes MySQL to treat enclosed data as strings and nonenclosed data as numeric.

- Removing all field delimiters (i.e., FIELDS TERMINATED BY '' ENCLOSED BY '') will cause a fixed-width format to be used. Data will be exported according to the display size of each field. Many spreadsheets and desktop databases can import fixed-width format files. You must have FILE permissions to execute this command.

The default behavior with no delimiters is to export tab delimited data using backslash (\\) as the escape character and to write one record per line. You may optionally specify a DUMPFILE instead of an OUTFILE. This syntax will cause a single row to be placed into the file with no field or line separators. It is used for outputting binary fields.

The list of tables to join may be specified in the following ways:

Table1, Table2, Table3, . . .

This is the simplest form. The tables are joined in the manner that MySQL deems most efficient. This method can also be written as Table1 JOIN Table2 JOIN Table3,... The CROSS keyword can also be used, but it has no effect (e.g., Table1 CROSS JOIN Table2) Only rows that match the conditions for both columns are included in the joined table. For example, SELECT * FROM people, homes WHERE people.id=homes.owner would create a joined table containing the rows in the people table that have id fields that match the owner field in the homes table.

Like values, table names can also be aliased (e.g., SELECT t1.name, t2.address FROM long_table_name t1, longer_table_name t2).

As of MySQL 5, it is better to use the standard ANSI SQL INNER JOIN syntax than this kind of join.

Table1 INNER JOIN Table2 {[ON expr] | [USING (columns)]}

Performs a standard inner join. This method is identical to the method just described, except you specify the USING clause to describe the join columns instead of a WHERE clause.

Table1 STRAIGHT_JOIN Table2

This is identical to the first method, except that the left table is always read before the right table. This should be used if MySQL performs inefficient sorts by joining the tables in the wrong order.

Table1 LEFT [OUTER] JOIN Table2 ON expression

This checks the right table against the clause. For each row that does not match, a row of NULLs is used to join with the left table. Using the previous example, SELECT * FROM people, homes LEFT JOIN people, homes ON people.id=homes.owner, the joined table would contain all the rows that match in both tables, as well as any rows in the people table that do not have matching rows in the homes table; NULL values would be used

for the homes fields in these rows. The OUTER keyword is
optional and has no effect.

Table1 LEFT [OUTER] JOIN *Table2* USING *(column[, column2 . . .])*

    This joins the specified columns only if they exist in both
tables (e.g., SELECT * FROM old LEFT OUTER JOIN new USING (id)).

Table1 NATURAL LEFT [OUTER] JOIN *Table2*

    This joins only the columns that exist in both tables. This
would be the same as using the previous method and specifying all the columns in both tables (e.g., SELECT rich_people.
salary, poor_people.salary FROM rich_people NATURAL LEFT
JOIN poor_people).

{OJ Table1 LEFT OUTER JOIN *Table2* ON *clause }*

    This is identical to *Table1* LEFT JOIN *Table2* ON *clause* and is
included only for ODBC compatibility.

MySQL also supports right joins using the same syntax as left
joins—except for the OJ syntax. For portability, however, it is
recommended that you formulate your joins as left joins.

If no constraints are provided, SELECT returns all the data in the
selected tables. You may also optionally tell MySQL whether to
use or ignore specific indexes on a join using USE INDEX and IGNORE
INDEX.

The search constraints can contain any of the following
substatements:

WHERE *statement*

    The WHERE statement construct is the most common way of
searching for data in SQL. This statement is usually a comparison of some type but can also include any of the following
functions, except for the aggregate functions. Named values,
such as column names and aliases, and literal numbers and
strings can be used in the statement.

FOR UPDATE

    Creates a write lock on the rows returned by the query. This
constraint is useful if you intend to immediately modify the
query data and update the database.

LOCK IN SHARE MODE

    Creates a shared mode lock on the read so that the query
returns no data that is part of an uncommitted transaction.

GROUP BY *column*[, *column2*,...]

This gathers all the rows that contain data with some value from a certain column. This allows aggregate functions to be performed on the columns (e.g., SELECT name,MAX(age) FROM people GROUP BY name). The column value may be an unsigned integer representing a column number or a formula, instead of an actual column name.

HAVING *clause*

This is the same as a WHERE clause except it is performed upon the data that has already been retrieved from the database. The HAVING statement is a good place to perform aggregate functions on relatively small sets of data that have been retrieved from large tables. This way, the function does not have to act upon the whole table, only the data that has already been selected (e.g., SELECT name,MAX(age) FROM people GROUP BY name HAVING MAX(age)>80).

ORDER BY *column* [*ASC*|*DESC*][, *column2* [*ASC*|*DESC*],...]

Sorts the returned data using the given column(s). If DESC is present, the data is sorted in descending order, otherwise ascending order is used (e.g., SELECT name, age FROM people ORDER BY age DESC). Ascending order can also be explicitly stated with the ASC keyword. As with GROUP BY, the column value may be an unsigned integer or a formula (though not an aggregate), instead of the column name.

LIMIT [*start*,] *rows*

Returns only the specified number of rows. If the start value is supplied, that many rows are skipped before the data is returned. The first row is number 1 (e.g., SELECT url FROM links LIMIT 5,10 returns URLs numbered 5 through 14).

PROCEDURE *name* ([*arg_list*])

In early versions of MySQL, this does not do anything. It was provided to make importing data from other SQL servers easier. Starting with MySQL 3.22, this substatement lets you specify a procedure that modifies the query result before returning it to the client.

SELECT supports functions. MySQL defines several built-in functions that can operate on the data in the table, returning the computed value(s) to the user. With some functions, the value returned depends on whether the user wants to receive a numerical or string value. This is regarded as the "context" of the function. When selecting values to be displayed to the user, only text context is used, but when selecting data to be inserted into a field, or to be used as the argument of another function, the context depends upon what the receiver is expecting. For instance, selecting data to be inserted into a numerical field will place the function into a numerical context.

MySQL 4.0 introduced support for unions. A UNION clause enables the results from two SELECT statements to be joined as a single result set. The two queries should have columns that match in type and number. Matching in type allows for columns to have types that are convertible.

MySQL 5.0 added the ability to create stored procedures and leverage the SELECT statement in those stored procedures. You can place result set data into stored procedure variables using the SELECT INTO @*variable* variant.

Examples

```
# Find all names in the 'people' table where the 'state'
Sfield is 'MI'.
SELECT name FROM people WHERE state='MI'
# Display all of the data in the 'mytable' table.
SELECT * FROM mytable
# Create a stored procedure that prints the number of rows
in a table
CREATE PROCEDURE counter (OUT p INT)
BEGIN
    SELECT COUNT(*) INTO p FROM account;
END;
```

SET

SET OPTION SQL_OPTION=*value*

Defines an option for the current session. Values set by this statement are not in effect anywhere but the current connection, and they disappear at the end of the connection. The following options are currently supported:

AUTOCOMMIT=0 or 1

When set to the default value of 1, each statement sent to the database is automatically committed unless preceded by BEGIN. Otherwise, you need to send a COMMIT or ROLLBACK to end a transaction.

CHARACTER SET *charsetname* or DEFAULT

Changes the character set used by MySQL. Specifying DEFAULT will return to the original character set.

LAST_INSERT_ID=*number*

Determines the value returned from the LAST_INSERT_ID( ) function.

PASSWORD=PASSWORD('password')

Sets the password for the current user.

PASSWORD FOR user = PASSWORD('password')

Sets the password for the specified user.

SQL_AUTO_IS_NULL= 0 or 1

When set to the default value of 1, you can find the last inserted row in a table with WHERE auto_increment_column IS NULL.

SQL_BIG_SELECTS=0 or 1

Determines the behavior when a large SELECT query is encountered. If set to 1, MySQL will abort the query with an error, if the query would probably take too long to compute. MySQL decides that a query will take too long if it will have to examine more rows than the value of the max_join_size server variable. The default value of the variable is 0, which allows all queries.

SQL_BIG_TABLES=0 or 1

Determines the behavior of temporary tables (usually generated when dealing with large data sets). If this value is 1, temporary tables are stored on disk, which is slower than primary memory but can prevent errors on systems with low memory. The default value is 0, which stores temporary tables in RAM.

SQL_BUFFER_RESULT=0 or 1

A value of 1 is the same as specifying SQL_BUFFER_RESULT for every SELECT statement. It forces MySQL to place results into a temporary table.

SQL_LOG_OFF=0 or 1

When set to 1, turns off standard logging for the current session. This does not stop logging to the ISAM log or the update log. You must have PROCESS LIST (SUPER as of MySQL 4.0.2) privileges to use this option. The default is 0, which enables standard logging.

SQL_LOW_PRIORITY_UPDATES=0 or 1

> Tells MySQL to wait until no pending SELECT or LOCK TABLE READ is occurring on an affected table before executing a write statement.

SQL_MAX_JOIN_SIZE=value or DEFAULT

> Prohibits MySQL from executing queries that will likely need more than the specified number of row combinations. If you set this value to anything other than the default, it will cause SQL_BIG_SELECTS to be reset. Resetting SQL_BIG_SELECTS will cause this value to be ignored.

SQL_QUERY_CACHE_TYPE=value

> Tells MySQL not to cache or retrieve results (0 or OFF), to cache everything but SQL_NO_CACHE queries (1 or ON), or to cache only SQL_CACHE queries (2 or DEMAND).

SQL_SAFE_UPDATES=0 or 1

> Prevents accidental executions of UPDATE or DELETE statements that do not have a WHERE clause or LIMIT set.

SQL_SELECT_LIMIT=number

> The maximum number of records returned by a SELECT query. A LIMIT modifier in a SELECT statement overrides this value. The default behavior is to return all records.

SQL_UPDATE_LOG=0 or 1

> When set to 0, turns off update logging for the current session. This does not affect standard logging or ISAM logging. You must have PROCESS LIST (SUPER as of MySQL 4.0.2) privileges to use this option. The default is 1, which enables update logging.

TIMESTAMP=value or DEFAULT

> Determines the time used for the session. This time is logged to the update log and will be used if data is restored from the log. Specifying DEFAULT will return to the system time.

Example

```
# Turn off logging for the current connection.
SET OPTION SQL_LOG_OFF=1
```

SHOW

```
SHOW [FULL] COLUMNS FROM table [FROM database] [LIKE clause]
SHOW DATABASES [LIKE clause]
SHOW FIELDS FROM table [FROM database] [LIKE clause]
SHOW GRANTS FOR user
SHOW INDEX FROM table [FROM database]
SHOW KEYS FROM table [FROM database]
SHOW LOGS
SHOW MASTER STATUS
SHOW MASTER LOGS
SHOW [FULL] PROCESSLIST
SHOW SLAVE STATUS
SHOW STATUS [LIKE clause]
SHOW TABLE STATUS [FROM database [LIKE clause]]
SHOW [OPEN] TABLES [FROM database] [LIKE clause]
SHOW VARIABLES [LIKE clause]
```

Displays a variety of information about the MySQL system. This
statement can be used to examine the status or structure of almost
any part of MySQL, including many objects not shown in this list.

Examples

```
# Show the available databases
SHOW DATABASES;
# Display information on the indexes on table 'bigdata'
SHOW KEYS FROM bigdata;
# Display information on the indexes on table 'bigdata'
# in the database 'mydata'
SHOW INDEX FROM bigdata FROM mydata;
# Show the tables available from the database 'mydata'
# that begin with the letter 'z'
SHOW TABLES FROM mydata LIKE 'z%';
# Display information about the columns on the table
# 'skates'
SHOW COLUMNS FROM stakes;
# Display information about the columns on the table
# 'people' that end with '_name'
SHOW FIELDS FROM people LIKE '%\_name';
# Show the threads
SHOW PROCESSLIST;
```

```
# Show server status information.
SHOW STATUS;
# Display server variables
SHOW VARIABLES;
```

TRUNCATE

TRUNCATE TABLE *table*

Drops and recreates the specified table.

Example

```
# Truncate the emp_data table
TRUNCATE TABLE emp_data;
```

UNLOCK

UNLOCK TABLES

Unlocks all tables that were locked using the LOCK statement during the current connection.

Example

```
# Unlock all tables
UNLOCK TABLES
```

UPDATE

UPDATE [LOW_PRIORITY] [IGNORE] *table*
 SET *column=value*, ...
 [WHERE *clause*]
 [LIMIT *n*]

Alters data within a table. You may use the name of a column as a value when setting a new value. For example, UPDATE health SET miles_ran=miles_ran+5 would add five to the current value of the miles_ran column.

The WHERE clause limits updates to matching rows. The LIMIT clause ensures that only n rows change. The statement returns the number of rows changed.

You must have UPDATE privileges to use this statement.

Example

```
# Change the name 'John Deo' to 'John Doe' everywhere in
the people table.
UPDATE people SET name='John Doe' WHERE name='John Deo'
```

USE

```
USE database
```

Selects the default database. The database given in this statement
is used as the default database for subsequent queries. Other databases may still be explicitly specified using the `database.table.column` notation.

Example

```
# Make db1 the default database.
USE db1
```

Transaction Rules

In general, your transactions are defined by the current auto-
commit statement. The default autocommit state for MySQL
is 1—meaning all statements are committed as they are executed. You can change this state by issuing the following
command:

```
SET AUTOCOMMIT=0
```

Transactions take place when auto-commit is off or when a
series of statements is prefixed with a `START TRANSACTION`
command. When a transaction is in operation, statements
are queued with no impact to the database until one of three
things happens:

- A `COMMIT` command is executed, causing all changes from
  the statements to take force in the database.

- A `ROLLBACK` command is executed, discarding the effects
  of any commands prior to the last commit/rollback.

- A statement with an implicit commit is executed.

In addition, you can commit or rollback and simultaneously begin a new transaction when the AND CHAIN modifier is added to the COMMIT or ROLLBACK.

Statements that force an implicit commit (i.e., they act as if you executed a COMMIT just before you execute them) include: ALTER EVENT, ALTER FUNCTION, ALTER PROCEDURE, ALTER TABLE, BEGIN, CREATE DATABASE, CREATE EVENT, CREATE FUNCTION, CREATE INDEX, CREATE PROCEDURE, CREATE TABLE, DROP DATABASE, DROP EVENT, DROP FUNCTION, DROP INDEX, DROP PROCEDURE, DROP TABLE, LOAD DATA INFILE LOCK TABLES, RENAME TABLE, SET AUTOCOMMIT=1, START TRANSACTION, TRUNCATE TABLE, UNLOCK TABLES.

You can also set up save points via the SAVEPOINT command that enable you to rollback to a specific point in an otherwise long transaction.

Transaction isolation levels define the impact of your transaction (and any locks created by the transaction). You define a transaction isolation level prior to starting any transaction through the following command:

```
SET [GLOBAL | SESSION] TRANSACTION ISOLATION LEVEL
    {READ UNCOMMITTED | READ COMMITTED | REPEATABLE READ|
SERIALIZABLE }
```

The default transaction isolation with InnoDB is repeatable read.

Operators

MySQL offers three kinds of operators: arithmetic, comparison, and logical.

Rules of Precedence

When your SQL contains complex expressions, the subexpressions are evaluated based on MySQL's rules of precedence. Of course, you may always override MySQL's rules of precedence by enclosing an expression in parentheses.

1. BINARY, COLLATE
2. !
3. - (unary minus) ~ (unary bit inversion)
4. ^
5. * / % DIV MOD
6. + -
7. << >>
8. &
9. |
10. < <= > >= = <=> <> IN IS LIKE REGEXP
11. BETWEEN CASE WHEN THEN ELSE
12. NOT
13. && AND
14. || OR XOR
15. :=

Arithmetic Operators

Arithmetic operators perform basic arithmetic on two values.

+

Adds two numerical values.

-

Subtracts two numerical values.

*

Multiplies two numerical values.

/

Divides two numerical values.

DIV
Integer division.

%

Gives the modulo of two numerical values.

|

Performs a bitwise OR on two integer values.

^

Performs a bitwise exclusive OR on two integer values.

&

Performs a bitwise AND on two integer values.

<<

Performs a bitwise left shift on an integer value.

>>

Performs a bitwise right shift on an integer value.

Comparison Operators

Comparison operators compare values and return 1 if the comparison is true and 0 otherwise. Except for the <=> operator, NULL values cause a comparison operator to evaluate to NULL.

<> *or* !=

Match rows if the two values are not equal.

<=

Match rows if the left value is less than or equal to the right value.

<

Match rows if the left value is less than the right value.

>=

Match rows if the left value is greater than or equal to the right value.

>

Match rows if the left value is greater than the right value.

value BETWEEN *value1* AND *value2*

 Match rows if *value* is between *value1* and *value2*, or equal to one of them.

value NOT BETWEEN *value1* AND *value2*

 Match rows if *value* is not between *value1* and *value2*.

value IN (*value1*,*value2*,...)

 Match rows if *value* is among the values listed.

value NOT IN (*value1*, *value2*,...)

 Match rows if *value* is not among the values listed.

value1 LIKE *value2*

 Compares *value1* to *value2* and matches the rows if they match. The righthand value can contain the wildcard '%', which matches any number of characters (including 0), and '_', which matches exactly one character. Its most common use is comparing a field value with a literal containing a wildcard (e.g., SELECT name FROM people WHERE name LIKE 'B%').

value1 NOT LIKE *value2*

 Compares *value1* to *value2* and matches the rows if they differ. This is identical to NOT (value1 LIKE value2).

value1 REGEXP/RLIKE *value2*

 Compares *value1* to *value2* using the extended regular expression syntax and matches the rows if the two values match. The righthand value can contain full Unix regular expression wildcards and constructs (e.g., SELECT name FROM people WHERE name RLIKE '^B.*').

value1 NOT REGEXP *value2*

 Compares *value1* to *value2* using the extended regular expression syntax and matches the rows if they differ. This is identical to NOT (value1 REXEXP value2).

Logical Operators

Logical operators check the truth value of one or more expressions. In SQL terms, a logical operator checks whether its operands are 0, nonzero, or NULL. A 0 value means false, nonzero means true, and NULL means no value.

NOT *or* !

> Performs a logical not (returns true if the argument is false, NULL if it is NULL, and otherwise false). Note that ! has a higher precedence than NOT.

OR *or* ||

> Performs a logical or (returns true if any of the arguments are nonzero and non-NULL, NULL if any are NULL; otherwise, returns false).

XOR

> Performs a logical exclusive or. If either operand is NULL, this operator evaluates to NULL. Otherwise, it evaluates to true if one operand is true, otherwise false. a XOR b is logically equivalent to (a AND (NOT b) OR ((NOT a) AND b).

AND *or* &&

> Performs a logical and (returns false if any of the arguments are false, NULL if any are NULL; otherwise, returns true).

Functions

MySQL provides built-in functions that perform special operations.

Aggregate Functions

Aggregate functions operate on a set of data. These are usually used to perform some action on a complete set of returned rows. For example, SELECT AVG(height) FROM kids would return the average of all the values of the height field in the kids table. AVG( ), COUNT( ), and SUM( ) allow DISTINCT.

AVG(*expression*)

Returns the average value of the values in *expression* (e.g., SELECT AVG(score) FROM tests).

BIT_AND(*expression*)

Returns the bitwise AND aggregate of all the values in *expression* (e.g., SELECT BIT_AND(flags) FROM options). A bit will be set in the result if and only if the bit is set in every input field.

BIT_OR(*expression*)

Returns the bitwise OR aggregate of all the values in *expression* (e.g., SELECT BIT_OR(flags) FROM options). A bit is set in the result if it is set in at least one of the input fields.

BIT_XOR(*expression*)

Returns the bitwise XOR aggregate of all the values in *expression* with 64-bit precision.

COUNT(*expression*)

Returns the number of times *expression* was not null. COUNT(*) will return the number of rows with some data in the entire table (e.g., SELECT COUNT(*) FROM folders).

GROUP_CONCAT([DISTNCT] *expression* [ORDER BY {*column* | *expression*}] [SEPARATOR *sep*])

Provides a string that combines in order all the results marked by *expression*.

MAX(*expression*)

Returns the largest value in *expression* (e.g., SELECT MAX (elevation) FROM mountains).

MIN(*expression*)

Returns the smallest value in *expression* (e.g., SELECT MIN(level) FROM toxic_waste).

STDDEV_POP(*expression*)

Returns the standard deviation of the values in *expression* (e.g., SELECT STDDEV_POP(points) FROM data). Also supported are the old MySQL STD( ) and the Oracle STDDEV( ) function, which both use the same syntax but are not portable. STDDEV_POP( ) is new standard SQL, provided as of MySQL 5.0.3.

STDDEV_SAMP([*expression*])

Returns the sample standard deviation of *expression*.

SUM(*expression*)

Returns the sum of the values in *expression* (e.g., SELECT SUM(calories) FROM daily_diet).

VAR_POP(*expression*)

Returns the population standard variance of *expression*. This function considers the entire data set and not a sample. This function is new as of MySQL 5.0.3 and replaces the older, nonstandard VARIANCE( ).

VAR_SAMP(*expression*)

Returns the sample variance of *expression*.

General Functions

General functions operate on one or more discrete values. We have omitted a few rarely used functions with very specialized applications.

ABS(*number*)

Returns the absolute value of *number* (e.g., ABS(-10) returns "10").

ACOS(*number*)

Returns the inverse cosine of *number* in radians (e.g., ACOS(0) returns "1.570796").

ADDDATE(*date*, INTERVAL, *amount, type*)

Synonym for DATE_ADD.

ADDTIME(*when,amount*)

Adds the specified *amount* as a TIME expression to the TIME or DATETIME of *when*.

AES_DECRYPT(*encrypted, key*)

Decrypts the AES-encoded string *encrypted* using the specified *key*.

AES_ENCRYPT(*plain, key*)

Encrypts the *plain* string based on the specified encryption *key* using AES encryption. The default is 128-bit encryption. As of MySQL 5.0, MySQL's AES encryption is the most cryptographically strong encryption method in MySQL.

ASCII(*char*)

Returns the ASCII value of the given character (e.g., ASCII(h) returns 104).

ASIN(*number*)

Returns the inverse sine of *number* in radians (e.g., ASIN(0) returns 0.000000).

ATAN(*number*)

Returns the inverse tangent of number in radians (e.g., ATAN(1) returns 0.785398).

ATAN2(*X, Y*)

Returns the inverse tangent of the point (*X,Y*) (for example, ATAN2(-3,3) returns -0.785398).

BENCHMARK(*num, function*)

Runs *function* over and over *num* times and returns 0.

BIN(*decimal*)

Returns the binary value of the given decimal number (e.g., BIN(8) returns 1000). This is equivalent to the function CONV(decimal,10,2).

BIT_COUNT(*number*)

Returns the number of bits that are set to 1 in the binary representation of the number (e.g., BIT_COUNT(17) returns 2).

BIT_LENGTH(*string*)

Returns the number of bits in *string* (the number of characters times 8, for single-byte characters).

CASE *value* WHEN *choice* THEN *returnvalue* ... ELSE *returnvalue* END

Compares *value* to a series of *choice* values or expressions. The first *choice* to match the *value* ends the function and returns the corresponding *returnvalue*. The ELSE *returnvalue* is returned if no *choice* matches.

CAST(*expression* AS *type*)

Casts the *expression* into the SQL type noted by *type*.

CEILING(*number*)

Returns the smallest integer greater than or equal to *number* (e.g., CEILING (5.67) returns 6).

CHAR(*num1*[,*num2*,. . .])

Returns a string made from converting each number to the character corresponding to that ASCII value (e.g., CHAR(122) returns Z).

CHAR_LENGTH(*string*)

Provides the length of a string in characters.

CHARACTER_LENGTH(*string*)

Provides the length of a string in characters.

CHARSET(*expression*)

Provides the character set of the string *expression*.

COALESCE(*expr1*, *expr2*, ...)

Returns the first non-NULL expression in the list (e.g., COALESCE(NULL, NULL, 'cheese', 2) returns cheese).

COERCIBILITY(*expression*)

Provides a code that represents the collation coercibility of the string *expression*. Values are:

0

Explicit collation

1

No collation

2

Implicit collation

3

System constant

4

Coercible

5

Ignorable

COLLATION(*expression*)

Provides the collation associated with the string *expression*.

COMPRESS(*expression*)

Compresses the string *expression* into binary data using the compression library (such as zlib) compiled into MySQL. If no compression library was compiled into the system, this function will return NULL.

CONCAT(*string1*[,*string2*,*string3*,. . .])

Returns the string formed by joining together all of the arguments (e.g., CONCAT('Hi',' ','Mom','!') returns Hi Mom!).

CONCAT_WS(*sep, string1*, [*string2*, ...])

Returns all strings as a single string, separated by *sep*.

CONNECTION_ID( )

Returns the ID of the current connection.

CONV(*number, base1, base2*)

    Returns the value of *number* converted from *base1* to *base2*. *number* must be an integer value (either as a bare number or as a string). The bases can be any integer from 2 to 36. Thus, CONV(8,10,2) returns 1000, which is the number 8 in decimal converted to binary.

CONVERT(*expression,type*)

    Synonym for CAST( ).

CONVERT(*expression* USING *charset*)

    Converts the specified *expression* string in one character set to the character set specified by *charset*. For example, CONVERT('Some latin-1 string.' USING utf8).

CONVERT_TZ(*expression,from,to*)

    Converts the DATETIME *expression* from the specified *from* time zone to the specified *to* time zone.

COS(*radians*)

    Returns the cosine of the given number, which is in radians (e.g., COS(0) returns 1.000000).

COT(*radians*)

    Returns the cotangent of the given number, which must be in radians (e.g., COT(1) returns 0.642093).

CRC32(*expression*)

    Computes a cyclic redundancy check on *expression* and returns a 32-bit unsigned value, or NULL if the argument is NULL.

CURDATE( )

    Returns the current date. A number of the form YYYYMMDD is returned if this is used in a numerical context; otherwise, a string of the form 'YYYY-MM-DD' is returned (e.g., CURDATE( ) could return 2007-08-24).

CURRENT_DATE( )

    Synonym for CURDATE( ).

CURRENT_TIME( )
   Synonym for CURTIME( ).

CURRENT_TIMESTAMP( )
   Synonym for NOW( ).

CURTIME( )
   Returns the current time. A number of the form HHMMSS is
   returned if this is used in a numerical context; otherwise,
   a string of the form HH:MM:SS is returned (e.g., CURTIME( )
   could return 13:02:43).

DATABASE( )
   Returns the name of the current database (e.g., DATABASE( )
   could return mydata).

DATE_ADD(date, INTERVAL amount type)
   Returns a date formed by adding the given amount of
   time to the given date. The type element to add can be
   one of the following: SECOND, MINUTE, HOUR, DAY, MONTH,
   YEAR, MINUTE_SECOND (as "minutes:seconds"), HOUR_MINUTE
   (as "hours:minutes"), DAY_HOUR (as "days hours"), YEAR_
   MONTH (as "years-months"), HOUR_SECOND (as "hours:min-
   utes:seconds"), DAY_MINUTE (as "days hours:minutes")
   and DAY_SECOND (as "days hours:minutes:seconds").
   Except for those time elements with specified forms, the
   amount must be an integer value (e.g., DATE_ADD("1998-
   08-24 13:00:00", INTERVAL 2 MONTH) returns 1998-10-24
   13:00:00).

DATE_FORMAT(date, format)
   Returns the date formatted as specified. The format string
   prints as given with the following values substituted:

   %a
      Short weekday name (Sun, Mon, etc.)

   %b
      Short month name (Jan, Feb, etc.)

%D

   Day of the month with ordinal suffix (1st, 2nd, 3rd, etc.)

%d

   Day of the month

%H

   24-hour hour (always two digits, e.g., 01)

%h/%I

   12-hour hour (always two digits, e.g., 09)

%i

   Minutes

%j

   Day of the year

%k

   24-hour hour (one or two digits, e.g., 1)

%l

   12-hour hour (one or two digits, e.g., 9)

%M

   Name of the month

%m

   Number of the month (January is 1)

%p

   A.M. or P.M.

%r

   12-hour total time (including A.M./P.M.)

%S

   Seconds (always two digits, e.g., 04)

%s

   Seconds (one or two digits, e.g., 4)

%T

> 24-hour total time

%U

> Week of the year (new weeks begin on Sunday)

%W

> Name of the weekday

%w

> Number of weekday (0 is Sunday)

%Y

> Four-digit year

%y

> Two-digit year

%%

> A literal % character

DATE_SUB(date, INTERVAL amount type)

> Returns a date formed by subtracting the given amount of time from the given date. The same interval types are used as with DATE_ADD (e.g., SUBDATE("1999-05-20 11:04:23", INTERVAL 2 DAY) returns 1999-05-18 11:04:23).

DAYNAME(date)

> Returns the name of the day of the week for the given date (e.g., DAYNAME('1998-08-22') returns Saturday).

DAYOFMONTH(date)

> Returns the day of the month for the given date (e.g., DAYOFMONTH('1998-08-22') returns 22).

DAYOFWEEK(date)

> Returns the number of the day of the week (1 is Sunday) for the given date (e.g., DAY_OF_WEEK('1998-08-22') returns 7).

DAYOFYEAR(date)

> Returns the day of the year for the given date (e.g., DAYOFYEAR('1983-02-15') returns 46).

DECODE(*blob, passphrase*)

Decodes encrypted binary data using the specified pass-phrase. The encrypted binary is expected to be encrypted with the ENCODE( ) function:

```
mysql> SELECT DECODE(ENCODE('open sesame', 'please'),
'please');

+------------------------------------------------+
| DECODE(ENCODE('open sesame', 'please'), 'please') |
+------------------------------------------------+
| open sesame                                     |
+------------------------------------------------+
1 row in set (0.01 sec)
```

DEGREES(*radians*)

Returns the given argument converted from radians to degrees (e.g., DEGREES(2*PI( )) returns 360.000000).

DES_DECRYPT(*encrypted*, [*key*])

Decrypts the DES-encrypted string *encrypted* using the optional *key* string.

DES_ENCRYPT(*plain*,[*key*])

Encrypts the specified *plain* string using the option *key* string or number using DES encryption.

ELT(*number,string1,string2, . . .*)

Returns *string1* if *number* is 1, *string2* if *number* is 2, etc. A null value is returned if *number* does not correspond with a string (e.g., ELT(3, "once","twice","thrice","fourth") returns thrice).

ENCODE(*secret, passphrase*)

Creates a binary encoding of the *secret* using the *passphrase*. You may later decode the secret using DECODE( ) and the passphrase.

ENCRYPT(*string*[,*salt*])

Password-encrypts the given string. If a salt is provided, it is used to add extra obfuscating characters to the encrypted string (e.g., ENCRYPT('mypass','3a') could return 3afi4004idgv).

EXP(*power*)

Returns the number e raised to the given power (e.g., EXP(1) returns 2.718282).

EXPORT_SET(*num, on, off, [separator, [num_bits]]*)

Examines a number and maps the on and off bits in that number to the strings specified by the on and off arguments. In other words, the first string in the output indicates the on/off value of the first (low-order) bit of *num*, the second string reflects the second bit, and so on. Examples:

```
mysql> SELECT EXPORT_SET(5, "y", "n", "", 8);
```

```
+--------------------------------+
| EXPORT_SET(5, "y", "n", "", 8) |
+--------------------------------+
| ynynnnnn                       |
+--------------------------------+
1 row in set (0.00 sec)
```

```
mysql> SELECT EXPORT_SET(5, "y", "n", ",", 8);
```

```
+---------------------------------+
| EXPORT_SET(5, "y", "n", ",", 8) |
+---------------------------------+
| y,n,y,n,n,n,n,n                 |
+---------------------------------+
1 row in set (0.00 sec)
```

EXTRACT(interval FROM datetime)

Returns the specified part of a DATETIME (e.g., EXTRACT(YEAR FROM '2001-08-10 19:45:32') returns 2001).

FIELD(*string,string1,string2, . . .*)

Returns the position in the argument list (starting with *string1*) of the first string that is identical to *string*. Returns 0 if no other string matches *string* (e.g., FIELD('abe','george','john','abe','bill') returns 3).

FIND_IN_SET(*string,set*)

Returns the position of *string* within *set*. The *set* argument is a series of strings separated by commas (e.g., FIND_IN_SET ('abe', 'george, john, abe, bill') returns 3).

FLOOR(*number*)

Returns the largest integer less than or equal to *number* (e.g., FLOOR(5.67) returns 5).

FORMAT(*number,decimals*)

Neatly formats the given number, using the given number of decimals (e.g., FORMAT(4432.99134,2) returns 4,432.99).

FOUND_ROWS( )

When executing a SELECT with a LIMIT clause, this function returns the number of rows the SELECT would have returned absent the LIMIT clause.

FROM_DAYS(*days*)

Returns the date that is the given number of days (in which day 1 is Jan 1 of year 1) (e.g., FROM_DAYS(728749) returns 1995-04-02).

FROM_UNIXTIME(*seconds*[, *format*])

Returns the date (in GMT) corresponding to the given number of seconds since the epoch (January 1, 1970 GMT). For example, FROM_UNIXTIME(903981584) returns 1998-08-24 18:00:02. If a format string (using the same format as DATE_FORMAT) is given, the returned time is formatted accordingly.

GET_LOCK(*name,seconds*)

Creates a named user-defined lock that waits for the given number of seconds until timeout. This lock can be used for client-side application locking between programs that cooperatively use the same lock names. If the lock is successful, 1 is returned. If the lock times out while waiting, 0 is returned. All others errors return NULL values. Only one named lock may be active at a time during a single session. Running GET_LOCK( ) more than once will silently remove any previous locks. For example: GET_LOCK("mylock",10) could return 1 within the following 10 seconds.

GREATEST(*arg1, arg2*[, *arg3*, . . .])
Returns the numerically highest of all the arguments (for example, GREATEST(5,6,68,1,-300) returns 68).

HEX(*decimal*)
Returns the hexadecimal value of the given decimal number (e.g., HEX(90) returns 3a). This is equivalent to the function CONV(decimal,10,16).

HOUR(*time*)
Returns the hour of the given time (e.g., HOUR('15:33:30') returns 15).

IF(*test, value1, value2*)
If *test* is true, returns *value1*, otherwise returns *value2* (e.g., IF(1>0,"true","false") returns true).

IFNULL(*value, value2*)
Returns *value* if it is not null; otherwise, returns *value2* (e.g., IFNULL(NULL, "bar") returns bar).

INET_ATON(*ip*)
Provides the number representation of a numeric IP address (i.e., 192.168.1.1) in string form.

INET_NTOA(*num*)
Provides the numeric address in string form associated with the specified network *num*.

INSERT(*string,position,length,new*)
Returns the string created by replacing the substring of *string* starting at *position* and going *length* characters with the string *new* (e.g., INSERT('help',3,1,' can jump') returns he can jump).

INSTR(*string,substring*)

Identical to LOCATE except that the arguments are reversed (e.g., INSTR('makebelieve','lie') returns 7).

INTERVAL(*A,B,C,D, . . .*)

Returns 0 if *A* is the smallest value, 1 if *A* is between *B* and *C*, 2 if *A* is between *C* and *D*, etc. All values except for *A* must be in order (e.g., INTERVAL(5,2,4,6,8) returns 2, because 5 is in the second interval, between 4 and 6).

ISNULL(*expression*)

Returns 1 if the expression evaluates to NULL; otherwise, returns 0 (e.g., ISNULL(3) returns 0).

LAST_INSERT_ID( )

Returns the last value that was automatically generated for an AUTO_INCREMENT field (e.g., LAST_INSERT_ID( ) could return 4).

LCASE(*string*)

Synonym for LOWER( ).

LEAST(*arg1, arg2*[, *arg3,. . .*])

Returns the numerically smallest of all the arguments (for example, LEAST(5,6,68,1,-20) returns -20).

LEFT(*string,length*)

Returns *length* characters from the left end of *string* (e.g., LEFT("12345",3) returns 123).

LENGTH(*string*)

Returns the number of bytes in *string* (e.g., LENGTH('Hi Mom!') returns 7).

LOAD_FILE(*filename*)

Reads the contents of the specified file as a string. This file must exist on the server and be world readable. Naturally, you must also have FILE privileges.

LOCATE(*substring,string*[,*number*])

Returns the character position of the first occurrence of *substring* within *string* (e.g., LOCATE('SQL','MySQL') returns 3). If *substring* does not exist in *string*, 0 is returned. If a numerical third argument is supplied to LOCATE, the search for *substring* within *string* does not start until the given position within *string*.

LOG(*number*)

Returns the natural logarithm of *number* (e.g., LOG(2) returns 0.693147).

LOG10(*number*)

Returns the common logarithm of *number* (e.g., LOG10(1000) returns 3.000000).

LOWER(*string*)

Returns *string* with all characters turned into lowercase (e.g., LOWER('BoB') returns bob).

LPAD(*string,length,padding*)

Returns *string* with padding added to the left end until the new string is *length* characters long (e.g., LPAD(' Merry X-Mas',18,'Ho') returns HoHoHo Merry X-Mas).

LTRIM(*string*)

Returns *string* with all leading whitespace removed (e.g., LTRIM(' Oops') returns Oops).

MAKE_SET(*bits, string1, string2, ...*)

Creates a MySQL SET based on the binary representation of a number by mapping the on bits in the number to string values. The first string will appear in the output if the first (low-order) bit of *bits* is set, the second string will appear if the second bit is set, and so on. Example:

```
mysql> SELECT MAKE_SET(5, "a", "b", "c", "d", "e",
"f");

+--------------------------------------------+
| MAKE_SET(5, "a", "b", "c", "d", "e", "f") |
+--------------------------------------------+
| a,c                                        |
+--------------------------------------------+
1 row in set (0.01 sec)
```

`MASTER_POS_WAIT(log, position, [timeout])`

Blocks operations until a slave has completed its updates against the *log* file up to the specified *position*. You can provide an optional *timeout* value to time out the blocking.

`MD5(string)`

Creates an MD5 checksum for the specified string. The MD5 checksum is always a string of 32 hexadecimal numbers.

`MICROSECOND(expression)`

Provides the number of microseconds represented in the specified *expression*.

`MID(string,position,length)`

Synonym for `SUBSTRING( )` with three arguments.

`MINUTE(time)`

Returns the minute of the given time (e.g., `MINUTE('15:33:30')` returns 33).

`MOD(num1, num2)`

Returns the modulo of *num1* divided by *num2*. This is the same as the % operator (e.g., `MOD(11,3)` returns 2).

`MONTH(date)`

Returns the number of the month (1 is January) for the given date (e.g., `MONTH('1998-08-22')` returns 8).

`MONTHNAME(date)`

Returns the name of the month for the given date (e.g., `MONTHNAME('1998-08-22')` returns August).

`NOW( )`

Returns the current date and time. A number of the form YYYYMMDDHHMMSS is returned if this is used in a numerical context; otherwise, a string of the form 'YYYY-MM-DD HH:MM:SS' is returned (e.g., `NOW( )` could return 1998-08-24 12:55:32).

`NULLIF(value, value2)`

Return NULL if *value* and *value2* are equal, or else returns *value* (e.g., NULLIF((5+3)18,1) returns NULL).

`OCT(decimal)`

Returns the octal value of the given decimal number (e.g., OCT(8) returns 10). This is equivalent to the function CONV(decimal,10,8).

`OCTET_LENGTH(string)`

Synonym for LENGTH( ).

`ORD(string)`

Returns a numeric value corresponding to the first character in *string*. Treats a multibyte string as a number in base 256. Thus, an 'x' in the first byte is worth 256 times as much as an 'x' in the second byte.

`PASSWORD(string)`

Returns a password-encrypted version of the given string (e.g., PASSWORD('mypass') could return 3afi4004idgv).

`PERIOD_ADD(date,months)`

Returns the date formed by adding the given number of months to *date* (which must be of the form YYMM or YYYYMM) (e.g., PERIOD_ADD(9808,14) returns 199910).

`PERIOD_DIFF(date1, date2)`

Returns the number of months between the two dates (which must be of the form YYMM or YYYYMM) (e.g., PERIOD_DIFF(199901,8901) returns 120).

`PI( )`

Returns the value of pi: 3.141593.

`POSITION(substring,string)`

Synonym for LOCATE( ) with two arguments.

`POW(num1, num2)`

Returns the value of *num1* raised to the *num2* power (e.g., POWER(3,2) returns 9.000000).

POWER(*num1, num2*)

Synonym for POW( ).

QUARTER(*date*)

Returns the number of the quarter of the given date (1 is January–March) (e.g., QUARTER('1998-08-22') returns 3).

RADIANS(*degrees*)

Returns the given argument converted from degrees to radians (e.g., RADIANS(-90) returns -1.570796).

RAND([*seed*])

Returns a random decimal value between 0 and 1. If an argument is specified, it is used as the seed of the random number generator (e.g., RAND(3) could return 0.435434).

RELEASE_LOCK(*name*)

Removes the named lock created with the GET_LOCK function. Returns 1 if the release is successful, 0 if it failed because the current thread did not own the lock, and a null value if the lock did not exist. For example, RELEASE_LOCK("mylock").

REPEAT(*string,number*)

Returns a string consisting of the original *string* repeated *number* times. Returns an empty string if *number* is less than or equal to zero (e.g., REPEAT('ma',4) returns mamamama).

REPLACE(*string,old,new*)

Returns a string that has all occurrences of the substring *old* replaced with *new* (e.g., REPLACE('*black jack*','*ack*','*oke*') returns bloke joke).

REVERSE(*string*)

Returns the character reverse of *string* (e.g., REVERSE('my bologna') returns angolob ym).

RIGHT(*string,length*)

Synonym for SUBSTRING( ) with FROM argument (e.g., RIGHT("string",1) returns g).

ROUND(*number*[,*decimal*])

Returns *number* rounded to the given number of decimals. If no *decimal* argument is supplied, *number* is rounded to an integer (e.g., ROUND(5.67,1) returns 5.7).

RPAD(*string*,*length*,*padding*)

Returns *string* with *padding* added to the right end until the new string is *length* characters long (e.g., RPAD('Yo',5,'!') returns Yo!!!).

RTRIM(*string*)

Returns *string* with all trailing whitespace removed (e.g., RTRIM('Oops ') returns Oops).

SECOND(*time*)

Returns the seconds of the given time (e.g., SECOND('15:33:30') returns 30).

SEC_TO_TIME(*seconds*)

Returns the number of hours, minutes, and seconds in the given number of seconds. A number of the form HHMMSS is returned if this is used in a numerical context; otherwise, a string of the form HH:MM:SS is returned (e.g., SEC_TO_TIME(3666) returns 01:01:06)

SESSION_USER( )

Synonym for USER( ).

SHA(*expression*)

Returns an SHA-1 checksum string for the specified *expression*.

SIGN(*number*)

Returns -1 if *number* is negative, 0 if it's zero, or 1 if it's positive (e.g., SIGN(4) returns 1).

SIN(*radians*)

Returns the sine of the given number, which is in radians (e.g., SIN(2*PI( )) returns 0.000000).

SLEEP(*seconds*)

Pauses the operation of the current SQL for the specified number of *seconds*.

SOUNDEX(*string*)

Returns the Soundex code associated with string (e.g., SOUNDEX('Jello') returns J400).

SPACE(*number*)

Returns a string that contains *number* spaces (e.g., SPACE(5) returns "   ").

SQRT(*number*)

Returns the square root of *number* (e.g., SQRT(16) returns 4.000000).

STRCMP(*string1*, *string2*)

Returns 0 if the strings are the same, -1 if *string1* would sort before *string2*, or 1 if *string1* would sort after *string2* (e.g., STRCMP('bob','bobbie') returns -1).

SUBDATE(*date*, INTERVAL*amounttype*)

Synonym for DATE_SUB( ).

SUBSTRING(*string*,*position*)

SUBSTRING(*string* FROM *position*)

Returns the remaining substring from *string* starting at *position*.

SUBSTRING(*string*,*position*,*length*)

SUBSTRING(*string* FROM *position* FOR *length*)

Returns a substring of *string* starting at *position* for *length* characters (e.g., SUBSTRING("123456",3) returns 3456).

SUBSTRING_INDEX(*string*,*char*,*number*)

Returns the substring formed by counting *number* of *char* within *string* and then returns everything to the left if the count is positive, or everything to the right if the count is negative (e.g., SUBSTRING_INDEX('1,2,3,4,5',',',3) returns "1,2,3").

SYSDATE( )

Similar to NOW( ), except it provides the time at which the function executes (whereas NOW( ) returns the time at which the query began).

SYSTEM_USER( )

Synonym for USER( ).

TAN(*radians*)

Returns the tangent of the given number, which must be in radians (e.g., TAN(0) returns 0.000000).

TIME_FORMAT(*time, format*)

Returns the given time using a format string. The format string is of the same type as DATE_FORMAT, as shown earlier.

TIME_TO_SEC(*time*)

Returns the number of seconds in the *time* argument (e.g., TIME_TO_SEC('01:01:06') returns 3666).

TO_DAYS(*date*)

Returns the number of days (in which day 1 is Jan 1 of year 1) to the given date. The date may be a value of type DATE, DATETIME, or TIMESTAMP, or a number of the form YYMMDD or YYYYMMDD (e.g., TO_DAYS(19950402) returns 728749).

TRIM([BOTH|LEADING|TRAILING] [*remove*] [FROM] *string*)

With no modifiers, returns *string* with all trailing and leading whitespace removed. You can specify to remove the leading or trailing whitespace, or both. You can also specify a character other than space to be removed (e.g., TRIM(both '-' from '---look   here---') returns look here).

TRUNCATE(*number, decimals*)

Returns *number* truncated to the given number of decimals (for example, TRUNCATE(3.33333333,2) returns 3.33).

UCASE(*string*)

Synonym for UPPER( ).

UNCOMPRESS(*compressed*)

Uncompresses the binary value *compressed*.

UNCOMPRESS_LENGTH(*compressed*)

Returns the uncompressed length of the specified *compressed* binary data.

UNHEX(*string*)

Performs the reverse operation of HEX( ).

UNIX_TIMESTAMP([*date*])

Returns the number of seconds from the epoch (January 1, 1970 GMT) to the given date (in GMT). If no date is given, the number of seconds to the current date is used (e.g., UNIX_TIMESTAMP('1998-08-24 18:00:02') returns 903981584).

UPPER(*string*)

Returns *string* with all characters turned into uppercase (e.g., UPPER ('Scooby') returns SCOOBY).

USER( )

Returns the name of the current user.

UTC_DATE( )

Returns the current UTC date as either a string or number ('2007-04-05' or 20070405) depending on whether the function is executed in a string or numeric context.

UTC_TIME( )

Returns the current UTC time as either a string or number ('11:04:03' or 110403) depending on whether the function is executed in a string or numeric context.

UTC_TIMESTAMP( )

Returns the current UTC timestamp as either a string or number ('2007-04-05 11:04:03' or 20070405110403) depending on whether the function is executed in a string or numeric context.

UUID( )
>   Returns a universally unique identifier that is guaranteed
>   to be unique across any two calls, even if the calls are
>   done on different machines using different versions of
>   MySQL using different operating systems.

VERSION( )
>   Provides the installed MySQL version.

WEEK(*date*)
>   Returns the week of the year for the given date (e.g.,
>   WEEK('1998-12-29') returns 52).

WEEKDAY(*date*)
>   Returns the numeric value of the day of the week for the
>   specified date. Day numbers start with Monday as 0 and
>   end with Sunday as 6.

WEEKOFYEAR(*date*)
>   Returns the week of the year (1–53) in which the date
>   represented by *date* takes place.

YEAR(*date*)
>   Returns the year of the given date (e.g., YEAR('1998-12-
>   29') returns 1998).

YEARWEEK(*date*)
>   Returns the year and week for the specified date value:
>   for instance, 200716.

Storage Engines

Table 5 lists some of the table types supported in most
MySQL installations. For truly atomic database transactions, you should use InnoDB tables. New transactional storage engines are being introduced at the time of this writing,
however.

Table 5. MySQL table types

Type	Transactional	Description
ARCHIVE	No	Used for archiving databases without indexes in a very small footprint.
BLACKHOLE	No	Stores no data at all. All queries return no rows.
CSV	No	Stores data in comma-separated files.
FALCON	Yes	New experimental, transactional storage engine to potentially replace InnoDB in a future release.
INNODB	Yes	Transaction-safe tables with row locking.
MEMORY (formerly HEAP)	No	Memory-based table; not persistent.
MERGE	No	A collection of MyISAM tables merged as a single table.
MYISAM	No	A newer, portable table type to replace ISAM.
NDB	Yes	Clustered storage engine for MySQL Cluster.

Stored Procedures and Functions

Stored routines are encapsulated SQL components that are stored in the database for reuse in your database applications. MySQL supports two kinds of stored routines: procedures and functions. They behave very similarly except for three key differences:

1. Functions accept only IN parameters; procedures can accept IN, OUT, and INOUT parameters.

2. Functions return a value; procedures return values via OUT or INOUT parameters.

3. Functions may be called in a query just like MySQL functions or user-defined functions; procedures are called independently via the CALL command.

The CREATE PROCEDURE/CREATE FUNCTION command creates a stored procedure. You must have CREATE ROUTINE privileges in order to create any stored procedure in MySQL. You must define a name and a body for the procedure:

```
CREATE PROCEDURE sitecount( )  SELECT COUNT(*) FROM web_
site;
```

You may subsequently call the procedure using the CALL command:

```
CALL sitecount( );
```

Parameters

MySQL supports three kinds of stored procedure parameters:

IN

> The parameter is passed into the procedure as input. The procedure can then operate on the parameter values. By default, a parameter is an IN parameter. Stored functions can accept only IN parameters.

OUT

> An output value is stored in the parameter for use by the caller of the stored procedure.

INOUT

> The caller passes into the procedure a value for the INOUT parameter and any changes made by the procedure then become available to the caller after the procedure is executed.

Parameters are specified in the procedure definition as a comma-separated list of parameters:

```
CREATE PROCEDURE sitecount(OUT total INT) SELECT COUNT(*)
INTO total FROM web_site;
```

```
CREATE PROCEDURE ssl_port(IN addr VARCHAR(255), OUT total
INT)
SELECT ssl_port INTO total FROM web_site WHERE address =
addr;
```

For each parameter, you may specify what kind of parameter it is, the name of the parameter, and the SQL type that it should store.

Pass parameters as a comma-separated list of values in the call:

```
CALL sitecount(@total);
SELECT @total;

CALL ssl_port('www.valtira.com', @port);
SELECT @port;
```

Logic

In additional to the simple logic described in the previous section, MySQL stored procedures allow complex application logic to be stored in the database. To perform complex logic, wrap the SQL in a BEGIN/END block:

```
DELIMITER //
CREATE PROCEDURE deactivate(IN pageId BIGINT)
BEGIN
UPDATE page SET active = 'N' WHERE page_id = pageId;
UPDATE content SET active = 'N' WHERE page = pageId;
END
//
```

Because the body can contain multiple statements that should end in the standard MySQL delimiter, you should define a temporary custom delimiter prior to creating the stored procedure.

Within a block, you can declare local variables using the DECLARE command:

```
DELIMITER //
CREATE PROCEDURE ssl_count(IN siteId BIGINT)
BEGIN
DECLARE total INT DEFAULT 0;
```

```
SELECT COUNT(*) INTO total FROM web_address
WHERE using_ssl = 'Y' AND web_site_id = siteId;
UPDATE web_site SET ssl_count = @total WHERE web_site_id =
siteId;
END
//
```

Finally, you can control the flow of procedure logic using the flow control commands common to most programming languages:

- IF THEN/ELSEIF THEN/ELSE/END IF
- CASE/WHEN THEN/ELSE/END CASE
- LOOP/END LOOP
- LEAVE
- ITERATE
- REPEAT/UNTIL/END REPEAT
- WHILE/DO/END WHILE

CASE

```
CASE [value]
WHEN expression THEN statements
[ELSE statements]
END CASE
```

Based on an optional value, the statements executes for the WHEN expression that matches that value. If no value matches, the ELSE statements are executed. When no value is specified, the true WHEN values are executed.

Example

```
CASE @total
WHEN 0 THEN UPDATE web_site SET ssl_port = 0 WHERE web_
site_id = siteId;
ELSE UPDATE web_site SET ssl_port = 443 WHERE web_site_id
= siteId;
END CASE;
```

IF

```
IF expression THEN statements
[ELSEIF expression THEN statements]
[ELSE statements]
END IF
```

Defines the conditional execution of one or more *statements* based on the truth value of an *expression* or series of *expression* values.

Example

```
IF total > 0 THEN UPDATE web_site SET ssl_port = 443 WHERE
web_site_id = siteId;
ELSE UPDATE web_site SET ssl_port = 0 WHERE web_site_id =
siteId;
END IF;
```

LOOP

```
[label:] LOOP
statements
END LOOP [label]
```

Executes the *statements* repeatedly until the loop is exited via LEAVE. By labeling the loop, you can match potentially ambiguous beginning and ending points for loops. The labels are arbitrary, but they must match each other.

Example

```
DECLARE total INT DEFAULT 0;
counter: LOOP
SET total = total + 1;
IF total > 50 THEN LEAVE counter; END IF;
END LOOP counter;
```

LEAVE

```
LEAVE label
```

Exits the flow control operation labeled by *label*.

ITERATE

```
ITERATE label
```

Breaks the control of the flow control operation specified by label to start over again. This statement is analogous to "continue" in languages such as Java and C.

REPEAT

```
[label:] REPEAT
statements
UNTIL expression
END REPEAT [label]
```

Loops through statements repeatedly until the expression in the UNTIL clause evaluates true.

Example

```
DECLARE total INT DEFAULT 0;
counter: REPEAT
SET total = total + 1;
UNTIL total > 50
END REPEAT counter;
```

WHILE

```
[label:] WHILE expression DO
statements
END WHILE [label]
```

Loops through statements repeatedly until the expression in the WHILE clause evaluates false.

Example

```
DECLARE total INT DEFAULT 0;
counter: WHILE total < 51 DO
SET total = total + 1;
END WHILE counter;
```

Cursors

Cursors enable you to operate on a set of results from a query one row at a time. Declare a cursor using the DECLARE command and associate it with a specific SQL query:

```
DECLARE site CURSOR FOR SELECT web_site_id FROM web_site;
```

Your procedure then fetches one row at a time from the cursor and executes logic based on data from that row:

```
DELIMITER //
CREATE PROCEDURE set_ssl()
BEGIN
DECLARE done INT DEFAULT 0;
DECLARE site_id BIGINT;
DECLARE total INT;
DECLARE site CURSOR FOR
SELECT web_site_id FROM web_site;
DECLARE CONTINUE HANDLER FOR SQLSTATE '02000' SET done =
1;
OPEN site;

REPEAT
FETCH site INTO site_id;
IF NOT done THEN
  SELECT COUNT(*) INTO total FROM web_address WHERE using_
ssl = 'Y';
  IF total > 0 THEN
    UPDATE web_site SET supports_ssl = 'Y' WHERE web_site_
id = site_id;
  ELSE
    UPDATE web_site SET supports_ssl = 'N' WHERE web_site_
id = site_id;
  END IF;
END IF;
UNTIL done
END REPEAT;

CLOSE site;

END
//
```

Handlers and Conditions

MySQL lets you know when a certain condition arises during the course of stored procedure processing through the use of handlers and conditions. The cursor example in the previous section included code that declared a handler to manage SQLSTATE '02000'—the end of the result set.

When declaring a handler, you define a handler type, what the handler is for, and the SQL to execute when the handler situation arises. MySQL supports the following types of handlers:

CONTINUE
> When the handler is executed, the SQL that generated it continues as if nothing happened.

EXIT
> After the handler is executed, execution terminates for the BEGIN/END block in which it was embedded.

UNDO
> Unsupported in MySQL.

The FOR clause of the handler declaration defines the circumstance under which the handler is called. You can specify any of the following scenarios:

- SQLSTATE error codes
- Your own custom conditions
- Shorthands for SQLSTATE codes to match: NOT FOUND, SQLWARNING, SQLEXCEPTION

Defining your own custom conditions consists of setting up simple names for specific SQLSTATE codes you are trying to handle; you can then subsequently use those conditions in handlers:

```
DECLARE THEEND CONDITION FOR SQLSTATE '02000';
DECLARE CONTINUE HANDLER FOR THEEND SET done = 1;
```

Triggers

Like a stored procedure, a trigger is processing logic stored in the database. Where a stored procedure executes in response to a specific application request, a trigger executes whenever a particular database event occurs. For any given event, you can define a trigger to execute BEFORE or AFTER the event. The events on which you can build a trigger are:

INSERT
> The trigger will execute whenever a row is inserted into the database.

UPDATE
> The trigger will execute whenever a row is updated in the database.

DELETE
> The trigger will execute whenever a row is deleted from the database.

Trigger definition works much like stored procedure definition in that your logic can be made up of compound SQL nested inside a BEGIN/END block. The main difference is that your logic is also bounded by a FOR EACH ROW section:

```
DELIMITER //
CREATE TRIGGER zap_addresses AFTER DELETE ON web_site
FOR EACH ROW BEGIN
DELETE FROM web_address WHERE web_site_id = OLD.web_site_
id;
END;
```

The special identifiers NEW and OLD reference the new and old row values, respectively.

Index

We'd like to hear your suggestions for improving our indexes. Send email to
index@oreilly.com.

Better than e-books

Buy *MySQL Pocket Reference*, 2nd Edition,
and access the digital edition FREE on
Safari for 45 days.

Go to www.oreilly.com/go/safarienabled
and type in coupon code NPPTIVH

Search
thousands of
top tech books

Download
whole chapters

Cut and Paste
code examples

Find
answers fast

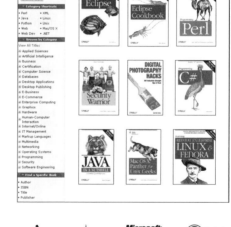

The premier electronic
reference library for
programmers and
IT professionals.

The O'Reilly Advantage

Stay Current and Save Money

Order books online:
www.oreilly.com/order_new

Questions about our
products or your order:
order@oreilly.com

Join our email lists Sign up
to get topic specific email
announcements or new
books, conferences, special
offers and technology news
elists@oreilly.com

For book content
technical questions:
booktech@oreilly.com

To submit new book
proposals to our editors:
proposals@oreilly.com

Contact us:
O'Reilly Media, Inc.
1005 Gravenstein Highway N.
Sebastopol, CA U.S.A. 95472
707-827-7000 or
800-998-9938
www.oreilly.com

Did you know that if you
register your O'Reilly books,
you'll get automatic notificatio
and upgrade discounts on
new editions?

**And that's not all! Once you've
registered your books you can:**

» Win free books, T-shirts and O'Reilly Ge

» Get special offers available only to
registered O'Reilly customers

» Get free catalogs announcing all our
new titles (US and UK Only)

**Registering is easy! Just go t
www.oreilly.com/go/registe**

O'REILLY®